patterns

mar

D1365135

graphs charts

FLASH
FORWARD
TEST PREP

spelling context

Written by **Kathy Furgang**

Illustrations by **Hector Borlasca**

Cover illustration by Hector Borlasca
Cover design by Loira Walsh
Interior design by Gladys Lai
Edited by Eliza Berkowitz

Flash Kids
A Division of Barnes & Noble
122 Fifth Avenue
New York, NY 10011

ISBN: 978-1-4114-1617-8

Please submit all inquiries to FlashKids@bn.com

Printed and bound in the United States

1 3 5 7 9 10 8 6 4 2

Dear Parent,

Test taking can be challenging for kids. In the face of test questions, answer bubbles, and the ticking clock, it's easy to see why tests can be overwhelming. That's why it's vital that children prepare for tests beforehand. Knowing the material is only part of preparing for tests. It's equally important that children practice answering different types of questions, filling in answers, and pacing themselves through test material. Children who practice taking tests develop confidence and can relax during the real test.

This Flash Forward Test Prep book will give your child the opportunity to practice taking tests in reading and math. Each practice test is based on national standards, so you know your child is reviewing important material he or she should be learning in the third grade. In addition to reinforcing third-grade curriculum, this book allows your child to practice answering different kinds of test questions. Best of all, each unit ends with a four-page practice test that reviews all the material in that unit. This truly gives kids a chance to show what they know and to see their progress.

The more practice children have before taking a test, the more relaxed and confident they will be during the exam. As your child works through the book, he or she will start to develop test-taking strategies. These strategies can be utilized during a real test. By the time your child finishes the book, he or she will be ready to tackle any exam, from the annual standardized test to the weekly pop quiz!

Table of Contents

Unit 2: Math

Test-Taking Tips

Preparing for a test starts with your mind and body. Here are some things you can do before the test to make sure you're ready.

- A few days before the test, get together with friends from your class to review the material. Have fun quizzing each other.

- The night before the test, go to bed early and get plenty of sleep.

- Eat a healthy breakfast the morning of the test.

- Find out beforehand if you need a pencil, eraser, or pen, and make sure you pack them in your schoolbag.

- Before you leave for school, do a few practice test questions at home to get warmed up.

- Remember to use the restroom before the test begins.

- Have confidence in yourself. A positive attitude will help you do well!

Once the test has started, you need to stay focused. Here are some tips to keep in mind during the test.

- Always begin by reading or listening carefully to the directions.

- Make sure you read all the answer choices before choosing the one you think is correct.

- If you get stuck on a certain question, it's okay to skip it. Go back to the question later.

- Work at your own pace. Don't pay attention to how quickly other students are completing the test.

- Fill in the answer bubbles completely and neatly.

- If you finish the test before time is up, use the time to review your answers.

- Take time to double check any questions you felt uncertain about. Make sure you want to stick with your answer.

Here are some tips to keep in mind when taking reading and language tests.

- Read each question or passage slowly and carefully.

- Say words in your head and think about the sounds.

- Underline important words in the question that tell you what you need to do.

- As you read a passage, underline key words and phrases.

- Use context clues to help figure out the meaning of a word you might not know.

- Cross out answers you know are wrong. Then focus on the remaining choices.

- It's okay to go back to the passage or sentence and reread it.

These tips will help you as you work on math tests.

- Find out if you can use a piece of scratch paper or part of the test booklet to work through math problems.

- Make sure you understand each question before you choose an answer. Reread the question if you need to.

- Solve a problem twice and make sure you get the same answer both times.

- Try plugging in the answer choices to see which one makes a true math sentence.

- When you're solving word problems or story problems, underline key words that tell you what to do.

- Draw a picture to help you visualize the right answer.

- Pay attention to the operation signs and make sure you know if you need to add, subtract, multiply, or divide.

Section 1: Reading
Main Idea

Read the story and answer the questions.

Save the Earth!

My name is Justin. I just finished a cool project for school. I designed a video game called Save the Earth. In the game, a player and up to three friends can go on adventures to different places on earth. The goal of the game is to help fix problems in the environment that were created by humans. The game will teach people to be more responsible with how they treat the earth.

As the game is played, the player will move on to harder and harder challenges. One challenge is to pick up litter. Another challenge is to help endangered plants and animals survive. I just wish this were a real video game I could play!

1. What is the main idea of the story?
Ⓐ Justin plays himself in a video game.
Ⓑ Justin is allowed to play video games at school.
Ⓒ Justin designed his own video game.
Ⓓ Justin wants to save the earth.

2. Which detail **best** helps to support the main idea?
Ⓐ Justin wishes he could play the game.
Ⓑ The players fix problems in the environment.
Ⓒ The levels will get harder and harder.
Ⓓ Four friends can play at a time.

3. What is another good title for the story?
Ⓐ "Justin Saves the Earth"
Ⓑ "The Environment"
Ⓒ "Video Games"
Ⓓ "Justin's School Project"

4. What is the object of Justin's video game?
Ⓐ to help people play better games
Ⓑ to teach people to be more responsible with the earth
Ⓒ to advance to harder and harder levels
Ⓓ to pick up litter

Cause and Effect

Read the story and answer the questions.

Billy and the Waterslide

Billy goes to the swimming center every Tuesday and Thursday. There is a rule at the swimming center. It says that any person who cannot swim is not allowed to use the waterslide. This makes Billy sad. He can't swim, but he wants to use the slide. It looks like fun!

Billy will be allowed to use the waterslide once he passes a simple swimming test. Billy's mom signs him up for a swimming class. Once he takes the class and learns to swim, he will be able to use the waterslide. He can't wait to learn to swim!

1. What causes Billy to get upset in the story?
   Ⓐ He does not want to take a swimming class.
   Ⓑ He wants to take a swimming class.
   Ⓒ He wants to use the waterslide but it is closed for repair.
   Ⓓ He wants to use the waterslide but does not know how to swim.

2. What is the effect of the swimming center's rule?
   Ⓐ Billy cannot go on the waterslide.
   Ⓑ Billy gets upset.
   Ⓒ Billy's mom signs him up for a swimming class.
   Ⓓ all of the above

3. What do you think the effect of the swimming class will be?
   Ⓐ Billy will not learn how to swim.
   Ⓑ Billy will be able to use the waterslide.
   Ⓒ Billy will not want to swim anymore.
   Ⓓ Billy will ask the swimming center to change its rules.

4. Which of the following **most likely** caused the swimming center to make its rule?
   Ⓐ a need for rules
   Ⓑ a need for swimming classes
   Ⓒ a need for safety
   Ⓓ a need for swimmers

Evaluating Characters

Read the story and answer the questions.

The Treasure

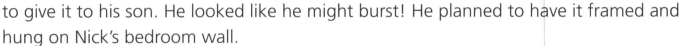

Nick's dad owns a store called Capital Comics. The store sells comic books. Nick loves when his dad brings home comics for him. Last week, Nick's dad came home with "The Amazing Spider-Man #23." This is a very rare Spider-Man comic book. Nick's dad was so excited to give it to his son. He looked like he might burst! He planned to have it framed and hung on Nick's bedroom wall.

Nick asked his dad if he could read the comic once before it was framed behind glass. Nick's dad read it to him before bed that night. The next day it was framed and hung in Nick's room. The comic means a great deal to Nick and his dad. Nick plans to keep it so he can give it to his own kids one day.

1. How do Nick and his dad feel about the Spider-Man comic?
   Ⓐ They both are happy to have it.
   Ⓑ Only Nick likes the comic.
   Ⓒ Only Nick's dad likes the comic.
   Ⓓ Neither of the characters are happy to have the comic.

2. Which statement **best** describes Nick's dad?
   Ⓐ He is not very kind to his son.
   Ⓑ He loves his son and wants to share things with him.
   Ⓒ He loves his son but is very strict with him.
   Ⓓ He is only interested in comics.

3. Which of Nick's actions shows that he likes the comic his dad brought him?
   Ⓐ It was Nick's idea to frame it and put it on the wall.
   Ⓑ Nick looked like he might burst when he saw it.
   Ⓒ Nick wanted to read it before it was framed behind glass.
   Ⓓ Nick wanted to show it to all of his friends.

4. Which word **best** describes Nick's feelings about comic books?
   Ⓐ bored
   Ⓑ excited
   Ⓒ angry
   Ⓓ confused

Problems and Solutions

Read the story and answer the questions.

Cindy's Decision

Cindy is going to be taking an after-school music class. She will have to pick a musical instrument to learn in the class. Once she chooses, she will have to stick with the instrument and practice in class and at home for a long time. The teacher told her that it might take years to play the instrument well.

After much debate, Cindy chose the flute. She picked it for several reasons. One was that she thought it sounded very beautiful. Her other consideration was that it was not too big. Some instruments, like the tuba and the drums, are very hard to carry around. Once her flute arrived, she was very happy and quickly got to work practicing. Cindy is enjoying learning how to play the flute.

1. What is Cindy's problem in the story?
   Ⓐ She does not want to be part of the music class.
   Ⓑ She is not allowed to be part of the music class.
   Ⓒ She has to choose an instrument to play.
   Ⓓ She does not like the instrument that she chose to play.

2. What other characters help Cindy solve her problem?
   Ⓐ Cindy's teacher
   Ⓑ Cindy's mother
   Ⓒ Cindy's sister
   Ⓓ No other characters help Cindy make her decision.

3. What helped Cindy solve her problem?
   Ⓐ She liked the sound of the tuba.
   Ⓑ She liked that a flute was easy to carry around.
   Ⓒ She thought the drums were too loud.
   Ⓓ Her mother did not want her to play the tuba or the drums.

4. What kind of conflict did Cindy have?
   Ⓐ a conflict with nature
   Ⓑ a conflict with other characters
   Ⓒ a conflict with herself
   Ⓓ a conflict with her schedule

Context Clues

Read the story and answer the questions.

Whiskers the Cat

Mrs. Freeley has a cat named Whiskers. Whiskers goes outside periodically. Mrs. Freeley sometimes leaves the window ajar and the cat is able to get out and explore the neighborhood. Usually Whiskers goes to places where she knows she can find food. Sometimes she finds some tuna at a house three blocks away. The woman who lives there puts out food for her.

This time Whiskers smells something new. It's coming from a restaurant nearby. She follows the smell and finds a damaged box of shrimp. The box cannot be used by the restaurant and is waiting to be picked up by the garbage collectors. While it sits, Whiskers gets a nice treat.

1. What does the word *periodically* mean?
Ⓐ always
Ⓑ sometimes
Ⓒ never
Ⓓ on Thursdays

2. What does the word *ajar* mean?
Ⓐ closed
Ⓑ open
Ⓒ cold
Ⓓ loud

3. What context clues help the reader find out the meaning of the word *damaged?*
Ⓐ The damaged box was found by a cat.
Ⓑ The damaged box had shrimp in it.
Ⓒ The damaged box could not be used by the restaurant.
Ⓓ The damaged box came from a restaurant.

4. What clue tells the reader that shrimp is a kind of food?
Ⓐ The smell of the shrimp is coming from a restaurant.
Ⓑ The box of shrimp is damaged.
Ⓒ Whiskers sees a box of shrimp.
Ⓓ The shrimp will be picked up by the garbage collectors.

Audience and Purpose

Read the passage and answer the questions.

An Actor's Life

Actors seem to have easy jobs. Although acting can seem fun, it is actually very hard work. It can take years of training before a person is considered a good actor. Actors in plays, films, and television have to study their lines. They have to understand how to say each line so that it makes sense to the story they are performing. They also have to concentrate. Performing is not easy work.

An actor has to remember to stay in character. If the actor does a good job, the audience will forget they are watching something that is not real. The work of an actor can be very rewarding. Anyone who wants to become an actor must remember that it will not always be fun or easy.

1. What is the author's purpose for writing the passage?
  Ⓐ to entertain the reader about acting
  Ⓑ to inform the reader about the difficulties of acting
  Ⓒ to persuade the reader to become an actor
  Ⓓ to persuade the reader not to become an actor

2. What kind of audience is the passage **most likely** meant for?
  Ⓐ someone who wants to become a teacher
  Ⓑ someone who is thinking about a career in acting
  Ⓒ someone who is about to go to the movies
  Ⓓ someone who likes hard work

3. What is the author's message?
  Ⓐ Acting is hard.
  Ⓑ Acting is fun.
  Ⓒ Acting is easy.
  Ⓓ Acting is boring.

4. What kind of writing **best** describes the passage?
  Ⓐ research paper
  Ⓑ how-to passage
  Ⓒ fiction story
  Ⓓ opinion article

Evaluating Information

Read the passage and answer the questions.

Internet Safety

Keeping safe on the Internet is very important. The same safety rules apply to Internet use as apply in real life. Strangers online are just like strangers on the street. You should not talk to strangers. You should only go to websites that you are familiar with or that you were told to go to. Don't wander off by yourself. Just like you shouldn't go down unfamiliar streets, don't go to websites you do not know. Also, do not buy anything on the Internet without permission from your parents. Internet safety is really a lot like everyday safety on the street.

1. What is the main idea of the passage?
Ⓐ Don't buy things on the Internet.
Ⓑ Don't talk to strangers on the street.
Ⓒ Street safety rules can also keep you safe on the Internet.
Ⓓ Get permission before you go down unfamiliar streets.

2. What does the author compare Internet safety with?
Ⓐ school safety
Ⓑ street safety
Ⓒ safety at home
Ⓓ website safety

3. Why do you think a stranger on the Internet is like a stranger on the street?
Ⓐ You can see what both of them look like.
Ⓑ You cannot see what either of them looks like.
Ⓒ You can tell that they want to harm you.
Ⓓ You cannot tell if they might want to harm you.

4. How can you wander off by yourself on the Internet?
Ⓐ by using an unfamiliar computer
Ⓑ by going to a website you are unfamiliar with
Ⓒ by going down a street you do not know
Ⓓ by using a website that you know well

Using Supporting Details

Read the passage and answer the questions.

The Future of the Sun

The sun powers life all around earth. It gives us heat and light. We couldn't live without it. Surprisingly, the sun is just like any other ordinary star in space. It seems so bright and powerful to us because it is the closest star to our planet.

Stars do not last forever. In about five billion years, our sun will explode. This is nothing to be alarmed by. It is quite common for stars to reach the end of their life. The sun is made of a gas called hydrogen. When a certain amount of the sun's hydrogen is used up, it will no longer have enough gravity to hold itself together. When this happens the sun will explode. The sun will then cool and glow a red color. It will be known as a red giant.

1. Which sentence **best** describes the main idea of the first paragraph?
   Ⓐ The sun powers life all around earth.
   Ⓑ It gives us heat and light.
   Ⓒ We couldn't live without it.
   Ⓓ Surprisingly, the sun is just like any other ordinary star in space.

2. Which detail in the first paragraph compares the sun to other stars?
   Ⓐ The sun powers life all around earth.
   Ⓑ It gives us heat and light.
   Ⓒ We couldn't live without it.
   Ⓓ Surprisingly, the sun is just like any other ordinary star in space.

3. What will happen that might cause the sun to explode?
   Ⓐ The sun will use up its light.
   Ⓑ The sun will use up its hydrogen.
   Ⓒ The sun will get weaker every year.
   Ⓓ The sun will slowly turn red.

4. Which detail is **most** important for understanding what might happen to the sun?
   Ⓐ Stars do not last forever.
   Ⓑ When a certain amount of the sun's hydrogen is used up, it will no longer have enough gravity to hold itself together.
   Ⓒ The sun is made of a gas called hydrogen.
   Ⓓ It seems so bright and powerful to us because it is the closest star to our planet.

Language Patterns

Read the poem and answer the questions.

Where's My Fiddle?

Hey, Diddle Diddle,
Have you seen my fiddle?
I want to play a song for the moon.
The last time I used it was on the tennis court.
I sure hope I find that fiddle soon!

1. Which word does the author rhyme with *Diddle?*
Ⓐ Hey
Ⓑ seen
Ⓒ fiddle
Ⓓ court

2. Which word does the author rhyme with *moon?*
Ⓐ Diddle
Ⓑ fiddle
Ⓒ court
Ⓓ soon

3. Which word is used mostly as a greeting?
Ⓐ Hey
Ⓑ Have
Ⓒ Diddle
Ⓓ soon

4. How many different sentence types are used in this poem?
Ⓐ 1
Ⓑ 2
Ⓒ 3
Ⓓ 4

Comparing and Contrasting

Read the passage and answer the questions.

Britain and the Colonies

In the early days of the colonies in America, things were peaceful. Although the colonies were far from Britain, they were under British rule. The colonies were like a home away from home. Colonists followed British laws. They paid taxes to Britain. They obeyed the British king, just like British citizens did.

Many colonists wanted to be free from British rule. By the late 1760s, many colonists wanted to create their own country. They did not want to pay taxes to Britain. They did not want to obey the king. Things changed as the two sides went to war. In the end, the colonies won their fight against the British. A new country was born.

1. How did the colonies and Britain compare in the early days?
   Ⓐ They both followed the same laws.
   Ⓑ They both obeyed the same king.
   Ⓒ They both paid taxes to Britain.
   Ⓓ all of the above

2. What two things are **not** being compared in the passage?
   Ⓐ British laws and colonial laws
   Ⓑ British soldiers and colonial soldiers
   Ⓒ life in the colonies and life in Britain
   Ⓓ taxes in the colonies and taxes in Britain

3. At the end of the war, how were Britain and the colonies alike?
   Ⓐ They both had the same king.
   Ⓑ They were both independent countries.
   Ⓒ They were located close to one another.
   Ⓓ They were both the same country.

4. How had the colonies changed by the end of the war?
   Ⓐ By the end of the war they agreed with the king.
   Ⓑ By the end of the war they no longer wanted to be free.
   Ⓒ By the end of the war they were independent.
   Ⓓ The colonies did not change by the end of the war.

Understanding Genre Features

Read the story and answer the questions.

The Fox and the Crow

One day, a crafty fox saw a crow in a tree. The crow was holding a cube of cheese in its mouth. The fox tried to think of a way to get that cheese for himself. Then he had an idea.

"Hello, Ms. Crow," said Fox. "You look so beautiful today. Your feathers are so shiny. You must be the most beautiful bird in this forest." Crow smiled. She was flattered by Fox's compliments.

"I'll bet your singing is just as beautiful as you are," said Fox. Crow smiled again. Just then, she opened her mouth to sing a beautiful bird song. When she opened her mouth, the cheese fell out and dropped right into Fox's open and waiting jaws.

"Foolish bird!" said the crafty fox.

1. What kind of story is this?
Ⓐ fairy tale
Ⓑ poem
Ⓒ fable
Ⓓ biography

2. What is the moral of the story?
Ⓐ Never eat cheese in a tree.
Ⓑ Never trust a crow.
Ⓒ Never trust someone who flatters too much.
Ⓓ Never compliment a bird.

3. Who are the characters in the story?
Ⓐ Fox
Ⓑ Crow
Ⓒ Fox and Crow
Ⓓ Fox, Crow, and Bird

4. How can you tell this is a fiction story?
Ⓐ It has dialogue.
Ⓑ It has facts and a plot.
Ⓒ It has facts and a setting.
Ⓓ It has talking animal characters.

Sequence

Read the passage and answer the questions.

Apple Pie Recipe

A great apple pie is easy to make. First, gather your ingredients. You will need a piecrust, eight apples, and two-thirds of a cup of sugar. You also need a quarter-cup of flour, a half-teaspoon of nutmeg, a teaspoon of cinnamon, and a little butter.

Peel and slice the apples and place them in a large bowl. Then mix all of the dry ingredients together. Mix them with the apples until everything is coated evenly. Pour the filling into the bottom crust. Add a few dabs of butter. Cover the pie with the top crust and pinch the edges closed. Cut a few holes in the top crust. Bake it in the oven at 375 degrees for 25 minutes. Enjoy!

1. What is the first thing to do when baking this pie?
Ⓐ Measure a quarter-cup of flour.
Ⓑ Peel eight apples.
Ⓒ Gather all of the ingredients.
Ⓓ Cut holes in the top crust.

2. Where do the apples go once they have been sliced?
Ⓐ in the oven
Ⓑ in a large bowl
Ⓒ in the piecrust
Ⓓ in the refrigerator

3. When do you use the butter?
Ⓐ before the apples are sliced
Ⓑ before the apples and dry ingredients are mixed
Ⓒ before the filling is poured into the piecrust
Ⓓ before the top crust is put on the pie

4. How long will it take to bake the pie?
Ⓐ about 35 minutes
Ⓑ about 25 minutes
Ⓒ about 15 minutes
Ⓓ about 5 minutes

Figurative Language

Read the story and answer the questions.

The Birthday Blues

It's my birthday today, but I feel as sick as a dog. I am dead tired and my head feels like it's going to explode. I stayed home from school today. Now I wish I could get out of bed and have some fun, but Mom is watching me like a hawk. She wants to make sure I don't strain myself.

Mom is taking care of me. Her chicken soup is a lifesaver. I've been eating it like there's no tomorrow. Mom wouldn't let me lay here like a lump on my birthday. She brought me some balloons and made her world-famous birthday cake. Now I feel like I can take on the world. There's no stopping the birthday boy now.

1. Which of the following phrases below is a figure of speech?
   - Ⓐ I stayed home from school today.
   - Ⓑ She brought me some balloons.
   - Ⓒ It's my birthday today.
   - Ⓓ Her chicken soup is a lifesaver.

2. Which of the following expressions is a metaphor?
   - Ⓐ I feel as sick as a dog.
   - Ⓑ I am dead tired.
   - Ⓒ Mom is watching me like a hawk.
   - Ⓓ I've been eating it like there's no tomorrow.

3. What do you think the title of the story means?
   - Ⓐ The person celebrating a birthday likes the color blue.
   - Ⓑ The person celebrating a birthday blew out the candles.
   - Ⓒ The person celebrating a birthday is feeling sad.
   - Ⓓ The person celebrating a birthday used blue to decorate for a party.

4. What does the saying "I've been eating it like there's no tomorrow" mean?
   - Ⓐ I will be eating it tomorrow.
   - Ⓑ I have been eating as if it's my last day on earth.
   - Ⓒ I have been eating as if tomorrow is my birthday.
   - Ⓓ By tomorrow we will be out of food.

Fact and Opinion

Read the passage and answer the questions.

Love a Penguin

Everybody loves penguins. They are one of the most interesting animals in the world. The penguin is a bird, but it doesn't fly. It uses its wings as flippers for swimming. It can use its webbed feet for walking on land. Sometimes penguins slide along the snow on their bellies. Penguins live mainly in the southern hemisphere. Many live in Antarctica, but some live farther north.

There are about 18 species of penguins. Many people like Emperor Penguins the best because they are the largest. A penguin's black and white feathers make it look like it is wearing a tuxedo. I wish I could have my own penguin as a pet.

1. Which is a fact from the passage?
   Ⓐ The penguin is a bird, but it doesn't fly.
   Ⓑ Everybody loves penguins.
   Ⓒ I wish I could have my own penguin as a pet.
   Ⓓ They are one of the most interesting animals in the world.

2. Which is an opinion from the passage?
   Ⓐ It uses it wings as flippers for swimming.
   Ⓑ Many people like Emperor Penguins the best because they are the largest.
   Ⓒ It can use its webbed feet for walking on land.
   Ⓓ Penguins live mainly in the southern hemisphere.

3. What fact can you find about Emperor Penguins?
   Ⓐ People like them the best.
   Ⓑ They make good pets.
   Ⓒ They are interesting animals.
   Ⓓ They are the largest penguin.

4. What body part **best** helps the penguin swim?
   Ⓐ its feet
   Ⓑ its wings
   Ⓒ its belly
   Ⓓ its head

Setting

Read the story and answer the questions.

My Room

My bedroom is my favorite place in the house. The walls are painted a bright pink. There are posters of horses, cats, and pandas all over the walls. I have a fuzzy purple rug that feels soft between my toes. It's not the biggest room in the world, but it's comfortable for me. I have a desk right next to my bed for doing homework. My desk has drawers for storing markers and construction paper. My bookshelf is filled with my favorite books and magazines. I could stay in this room all the time if I had to. Sure, I like to go outside to play, but my bedroom is a pretty fun place too.

1. How does the author describe the setting of her bedroom?
Ⓐ cluttered
Ⓑ boring
Ⓒ fun
Ⓓ neat

2. What do you think the author likes most about her room?
Ⓐ She can do her homework there.
Ⓑ She can sleep there.
Ⓒ All of her clothes are there.
Ⓓ All of her favorite things are there.

3. How do the posters help to add to the setting of the room?
Ⓐ They show what the author likes.
Ⓑ They show what the author dislikes.
Ⓒ They show what the author has to do for homework.
Ⓓ They show what the author's favorite sports are.

4. Why does the author say she could stay in her room all the time if she had to?
Ⓐ The room is a fun place to be.
Ⓑ The room is pretty.
Ⓒ The author has a lot of homework to do.
Ⓓ The author does not like to go outside.

Identifying Textual Features

Read the passage and answer the questions.

An American City

What do you think of when you think about the president of the United States? You might think of the White House in Washington, D.C. It has been the home of president after president for decades. The first president, George Washington, never lived in the White House we know today. At the time he was president, the White House had not yet been built. America's capital had not yet been built, either. In fact, Washington, D.C. was named after George Washington!

The city has an interesting history. It was planned and developed in the late 1700s. It is the place where our national government is run. The D.C. in Washington, D.C. stands for the District of Columbia. The name is meant to honor another important person in American history: Christopher Columbus.

1. How many paragraphs are in the passage?
Ⓐ 1
Ⓑ 2
Ⓒ 3
Ⓓ 4

2. What is the topic sentence of paragraph 2?
Ⓐ sentence 1
Ⓑ sentence 2
Ⓒ sentence 3
Ⓓ sentence 4

3. What kind of sentence is the first sentence of the passage?
Ⓐ exclamation
Ⓑ declaration
Ⓒ question
Ⓓ caption

4. What kind of punctuation mark is in the last sentence of the passage?
Ⓐ exclamation mark
Ⓑ question mark
Ⓒ colon
Ⓓ semi-colon

Making Inferences

Read the story and answer the questions.

Keisha Forgets

Keisha ran into the house dripping wet. Her umbrella was sitting inside the front door. "Why did I forget it?" she asked as she shook water drops from her hair.

"Well, take it now, honey," her mom said. "Don't be late! You only have another three or four minutes to get back down to the corner." Keisha did not like being late. Her mother didn't like it either.

"Bye, Mom," she yelled as the front door slammed behind her. "See you later!"

"OK," her mom called back. "I'll see you later."

As soon as Keisha left the house, her mom cleared the breakfast table, washed the dishes, and made the beds for the day.

1. Where do you think Keisha is going?
  Ⓐ to the doctor
  Ⓑ to school
  Ⓒ to the store
  Ⓓ to the kitchen

2. Why is Keisha wet?
  Ⓐ It is raining.
  Ⓑ She just took a shower.
  Ⓒ She forgot to dry her hair.
  Ⓓ She walked under a sprinkler.

3. What will happen at the corner in three or four minutes?
  Ⓐ School will start.
  Ⓑ It will stop raining.
  Ⓒ It will stop snowing.
  Ⓓ The school bus will stop.

4. How can you tell the story takes place in the morning?
  Ⓐ Keisha is forgetful in the mornings.
  Ⓑ Keisha would need an umbrella in the morning.
  Ⓒ Keisha's mother is clearing the breakfast table.
  Ⓓ Keisha's mother tells Keisha she will see her later.

Evaluating Nonfiction

Read the passage and answer the questions.

Recycling Helps

Think about all of the resources you use every day. You use glass and plastic bottles, metal cans, and paper. Did you know that Americans use more than 67 million tons of paper each year? It takes 98 tons of resources to make just one ton of paper. To help the earth, pay attention to how much paper you use. Use less if possible. Try to use both sides of the paper when you can. Don't forget to recycle, of course! Recycling paper saves trees.

Americans use a lot of plastic bottles too. In fact, they use 4 million plastic bottles an hour! And of these 4 million bottles, only 25 percent are recycled. Reuse plastic bottles when you can. Reducing waste can help our planet!

1. What is the main idea of the passage?
   Ⓐ You should recycle paper.
   Ⓑ You should recycle glass.
   Ⓒ Americans use a lot of plastic bottles.
   Ⓓ You should use fewer resources and recycle more.

2. How often do Americans go through 4 million plastic bottles?
   Ⓐ every year
   Ⓑ every week
   Ⓒ every day
   Ⓓ every hour

3. What percentage of plastic bottles are recycled?
   Ⓐ 15
   Ⓑ 25
   Ⓒ 30
   Ⓓ 60

4. What is one resource you are saving when you recycle paper?
   Ⓐ trees
   Ⓑ plastic
   Ⓒ metal
   Ⓓ soil

Responding to Literature

Read the story and answer the questions.

Tornado

Craig and his family listened to the weather report. Another tornado was headed their way. There was no time to lose. They ran down into their basement to wait it out again. This was the third tornado warning for their area in the past month.

Craig's sister always gets a little scared when tornado warnings come. Once, a tornado destroyed their aunt's entire house. Craig's sister is always afraid that the same thing will happen to their house too. And to tell the truth, Craig is a little frightened as well.

After waiting in their basement with flashlights and extra food and water, the warning passed. They were safe again.

1. Who is the narrator of this story?
   Ⓐ Craig
   Ⓑ Craig's sister
   Ⓒ Craig's aunt
   Ⓓ someone outside the story

2. What happens in the middle of the story?
   Ⓐ Craig and his family are safe from the tornado.
   Ⓑ Craig packs flashlights and extra food and water.
   Ⓒ Craig and his sister are afraid of the possible tornado.
   Ⓓ Craig and his family listen to the weather report.

3. What is the point of view of the story?
   Ⓐ first person
   Ⓑ second person
   Ⓒ third person
   Ⓓ fourth person

4. Who is the main character of the story?
   Ⓐ Craig
   Ⓑ Craig's sister
   Ⓒ Craig's aunt
   Ⓓ Craig's mother

Section 2:
Written and Oral Language Conventions
Phonics

Answer the questions below.

1. Which word below has a short *a* sound?
   - Ⓐ cake
   - Ⓑ caught
   - Ⓒ tap
   - Ⓓ tray

2. Which word below has a long *i* sound?
   - Ⓐ kit
   - Ⓑ flight
   - Ⓒ into
   - Ⓓ kitten

3. Which word below has a short *o* sound?
   - Ⓐ tooth
   - Ⓑ cottage
   - Ⓒ smooth
   - Ⓓ coat

4. Which word below does **not** have a consonant blend?
   - Ⓐ strength
   - Ⓑ boat
   - Ⓒ flight
   - Ⓓ play

5. Which word below has a short vowel sound?
   - Ⓐ valve
   - Ⓑ soap
   - Ⓒ try
   - Ⓓ night

6. Which word is in the same word family as *habit?*
   - Ⓐ hat
   - Ⓑ hate
   - Ⓒ rabbit
   - Ⓓ great

7. Which word is in the same word family as *valley?*
   - Ⓐ alley
   - Ⓑ silly
   - Ⓒ vacuum
   - Ⓓ van

8. Which word has the same vowel sound as *true?*
   - Ⓐ glue
   - Ⓑ umbrella
   - Ⓒ upset
   - Ⓓ tugboat

9. Which word has a silent *g?*
   - Ⓐ great
   - Ⓑ flight
   - Ⓒ twig
   - Ⓓ gladly

10. Which word has the fewest syllables?
    - Ⓐ recent
    - Ⓑ recess
    - Ⓒ smile
    - Ⓓ opening

Synonyms

Answer the questions below.

1. Which word has the same meaning as *under?*
- Ⓐ below
- Ⓑ above
- Ⓒ beside
- Ⓓ move

2. Which word has a meaning most similar to *special?*
- Ⓐ approved
- Ⓑ creative
- Ⓒ unique
- Ⓓ forgotten

3. Which word has a meaning most similar to *gravel?*
- Ⓐ sand
- Ⓑ dirt
- Ⓒ stones
- Ⓓ boulders

4. Which word has a meaning most similar to *prepare?*
- Ⓐ study
- Ⓑ burn
- Ⓒ carry
- Ⓓ gasp

5. Which word is a synonym for *gather?*
- Ⓐ deliver
- Ⓑ collect
- Ⓒ attempt
- Ⓓ mark

6. Which word has a meaning most similar to *grill?*
- Ⓐ clean
- Ⓑ cook
- Ⓒ chop
- Ⓓ create

7. Which word has a meaning most similar to *garbage?*
- Ⓐ paper
- Ⓑ glass
- Ⓒ trash
- Ⓓ can

8. Which word has the same meaning as *give?*
- Ⓐ show
- Ⓑ ask
- Ⓒ take
- Ⓓ present

9. Which word has a meaning most similar to the words *grateful* and *thankful?*
- Ⓐ sorrowful
- Ⓑ pleased
- Ⓒ forgetful
- Ⓓ welcome

10. Which word has the same meaning as *incredible?*
- Ⓐ special
- Ⓑ unhappy
- Ⓒ unbelievable
- Ⓓ funny

Antonyms

Answer the questions below.

1. Which word means the opposite of *frigid?*
   - Ⓐ warm
   - Ⓑ cold
   - Ⓒ hot
   - Ⓓ icy

2. Which word means the opposite of *bashful?*
   - Ⓐ shy
   - Ⓑ outgoing
   - Ⓒ confused
   - Ⓓ creative

3. Which word means the opposite of *quiet?*
   - Ⓐ rude
   - Ⓑ disobey
   - Ⓒ soft
   - Ⓓ loud

4. Which word means the opposite of *build?*
   - Ⓐ destroy
   - Ⓑ plan
   - Ⓒ make
   - Ⓓ attempt

5. Which word means the opposite of *clever?*
   - Ⓐ crafty
   - Ⓑ smart
   - Ⓒ original
   - Ⓓ unoriginal

6. Which word means the opposite of *receive?*
   - Ⓐ give
   - Ⓑ get
   - Ⓒ wrap
   - Ⓓ choose

7. Which word means the opposite of *begin?*
   - Ⓐ examine
   - Ⓑ look
   - Ⓒ end
   - Ⓓ start

8. Which word means the opposite of *release?*
   - Ⓐ watch
   - Ⓑ escape
   - Ⓒ catch
   - Ⓓ show

9. Which word means the opposite of *quick?*
   - Ⓐ fast
   - Ⓑ speedy
   - Ⓒ finished
   - Ⓓ slow

10. Which word means the opposite of *organized?*
    - Ⓐ disorganized
    - Ⓑ displayed
    - Ⓒ neat
    - Ⓓ dirty

Prefixes

Answer the questions below.

1. What is the prefix in the word *unbelievable?*
   - Ⓐ un
   - Ⓑ believe
   - Ⓒ believable
   - Ⓓ able

2. Which prefix means *out?*
   - Ⓐ non-
   - Ⓑ un-
   - Ⓒ ex-
   - Ⓓ pre-

3. Which prefix means *before?*
   - Ⓐ non-
   - Ⓑ un-
   - Ⓒ ex-
   - Ⓓ pre-

4. What prefix can you add to *sensitive* to mean *not sensitive?*
   - Ⓐ ex-
   - Ⓑ e-
   - Ⓒ pro-
   - Ⓓ in-

5. What is the prefix in the word *proactive?*
   - Ⓐ -tive
   - Ⓑ -act
   - Ⓒ active
   - Ⓓ pro-

6. What prefix can you add to *enter* to mean *enter again?*
   - Ⓐ non-
   - Ⓑ un-
   - Ⓒ re-
   - Ⓓ a-

7. Which prefix means *not?*
   - Ⓐ re-
   - Ⓑ ex-
   - Ⓒ in-
   - Ⓓ post-

8. How can you change the word *preview* to mean *to view again?*
   - Ⓐ change *view* to *look*
   - Ⓑ change pre- to un-
   - Ⓒ change pre- to re-
   - Ⓓ change *view* to *again*

9. What does the prefix *post-* mean?
   - Ⓐ in
   - Ⓑ out
   - Ⓒ before
   - Ⓓ after

10. What does the prefix *inter-* mean?
    - Ⓐ above
    - Ⓑ under
    - Ⓒ between
    - Ⓓ inside

Suffixes

Answer the questions below.

1. Where can the suffix of a word be found?
  Ⓐ at the beginning
  Ⓑ in the middle
  Ⓒ at the end
  Ⓓ in the word before it

2. What does the suffix –*ing* mean?
  Ⓐ in the process of
  Ⓑ having just finished
  Ⓒ about to begin
  Ⓓ in the distant past

3. What is the suffix in the word *incompletely?*
  Ⓐ in-
  Ⓑ com-
  Ⓒ complete
  Ⓓ -ly

4. What is the suffix in the word *organization?*
  Ⓐ or-
  Ⓑ -zation
  Ⓒ -ation
  Ⓓ -tion

5. If you change the suffix of *walking* to mean *done walking*, what word do you make?
  Ⓐ walkize
  Ⓑ walked
  Ⓒ walker
  Ⓓ walks

6. What does the suffix –*ist* mean?
  Ⓐ an action
  Ⓑ a person who
  Ⓒ in the past
  Ⓓ in the future

7. What does the suffix –*or* mean?
  Ⓐ an action
  Ⓑ a person who
  Ⓒ in the past
  Ⓓ in the future

8. What does *baker* mean?
  Ⓐ baked in the past
  Ⓑ will bake in the future
  Ⓒ someone who bakes
  Ⓓ to bake

9. What does *visible* mean?
  Ⓐ to see
  Ⓑ able to be seen
  Ⓒ saw
  Ⓓ seeing

10. What is the suffix in the word *bravery?*
  Ⓐ bra-
  Ⓑ brave
  Ⓒ -ery
  Ⓓ -y

Punctuation

Answer the questions below.

1. What kind of punctuation mark belongs at the end of the following sentence?

When did you finish your homework

Ⓐ period
Ⓑ exclamation point
Ⓒ question mark
Ⓓ semi colon

2. Which sentence would **most likely** get an exclamation point at the end?

Ⓐ Jake ate dinner
Ⓑ Why did Jake eat dinner
Ⓒ Can you believe that Jake made dinner
Ⓓ Jake made a wonderful dinner

3. Which sentence uses the correct punctuation?

Ⓐ "I wish I could come with you," said Sally.
Ⓑ I wish I could come with you, said Sally.
Ⓒ "I wish I could come with you." said Sally.
Ⓓ "I wish I could come with you, said Sally."

4. Where should a comma be placed in the following sentence?

I bought butter, eggs bread and flour.

Ⓐ after *eggs*
Ⓑ after *bread*
Ⓒ after *eggs* and *bread*
Ⓓ after *eggs*, *bread*, and *and*

5. Which of the marks below shows a closed quotation mark?

Ⓐ ?
Ⓑ !
Ⓒ "
Ⓓ "

6. Which is the correct way to write "the book that belongs to Kyle"?

Ⓐ Kyles book
Ⓑ Kyle's book
Ⓒ Kyles's book
Ⓓ Kyles book's

7. What kind of punctuation mark belongs at the end of the following sentence?

"Look out below!" she said

Ⓐ period
Ⓑ exclamation point
Ⓒ question mark
Ⓓ quotation mark

8. Which sentence is written correctly?

Ⓐ I was born on August 1 1997.
Ⓑ I was born on August, 1 1997.
Ⓒ I was born on August 1, 1997.
Ⓓ I was born, on August 1, 1997.

Capitalization

Answer the questions below.

1. Which word below should always be capitalized in a sentence?
Ⓐ she
Ⓑ look
Ⓒ america
Ⓓ horse

2. Which sentence is written correctly?
Ⓐ Let's meet on Main street.
Ⓑ Let's Meet on Main Street.
Ⓒ Let's meet on main Street.
Ⓓ Let's meet on Main Street.

3. Which word should be capitalized in the following sentence?
My mother was born in october.
Ⓐ mother
Ⓑ born
Ⓒ october
Ⓓ none of the above

4. Which sentence is written correctly?
Ⓐ tomorrow is saturday the 18th.
Ⓑ tomorrow is Saturday the 18th.
Ⓒ Tomorrow is Saturday the 18th.
Ⓓ Tomorrow is saturday the 18th.

5. Which of the following does **not** always get capitalized in a sentence?
Ⓐ the beginning letter
Ⓑ a person's name
Ⓒ the name of a street or town
Ⓓ a place

6. Which of the following should be capitalized in a sentence?
Ⓐ the football field
Ⓑ my school
Ⓒ memorial hospital
Ⓓ his car

7. Which of the following should **not** be capitalized in a sentence?
Ⓐ Baby
Ⓑ Donna
Ⓒ Raymond
Ⓓ Sasha

8. Which sentence shows the correct capitalization?
Ⓐ Miguel and rick will be at a party on Memorial Day.
Ⓑ Miguel and Rick will be at a party on Memorial Day.
Ⓒ Miguel and rick will be at a party on memorial day.
Ⓓ Miguel and Rick will be at a party on memorial Day.

Compound Words

Answer the questions below.

1. Which word below is a compound word?
- Ⓐ lightning
- Ⓑ snowing
- Ⓒ lighthouse
- Ⓓ important

2. Which compound word means "a shirt worn under another shirt"?
- Ⓐ shirtless
- Ⓑ coverall
- Ⓒ undershirt
- Ⓓ shirt

3. Which compound word means "bad weather involving snow"?
- Ⓐ snowflake
- Ⓑ snowman
- Ⓒ snowstorm
- Ⓓ snowweather

4. What two words make up the compound word *trustworthy*?
- Ⓐ *trust* and *wort*
- Ⓑ *trus* and *worth*
- Ⓒ *trust* and *worse*
- Ⓓ *trust* and *worthy*

5. Which word below is **not** a compound word?
- Ⓐ carefree
- Ⓑ careless
- Ⓒ postcard
- Ⓓ posting

6. What is the **best** definition for the word *evergreen*?
- Ⓐ always green
- Ⓑ always greedy
- Ⓒ every green
- Ⓓ never green

7. Which compound word does **not** have to do with people?
- Ⓐ everyone
- Ⓑ someone
- Ⓒ nobody
- Ⓓ sometime

8. What two words make up the compound word *classmate*?
- Ⓐ *class* and *ate*
- Ⓑ *class* and *mate*
- Ⓒ *last* and *ate*
- Ⓓ *classy* and *mate*

9. Which word below is a compound word?
- Ⓐ worthless
- Ⓑ ringing
- Ⓒ sadly
- Ⓓ inning

10. Which compound word means "beneath the ground"?
- Ⓐ groundless
- Ⓑ groundhog
- Ⓒ underground
- Ⓓ underneath

Multiple Meaning Words

Answer the questions below.

1. *Blue is a color.* What other meaning does *blue* have?
Ⓐ number
Ⓑ sad
Ⓒ great
Ⓓ artistic

2. *We dug coal from a mine.* What other meaning does *mine* have?
Ⓐ belonging to me
Ⓑ able to be seen through
Ⓒ below
Ⓓ belonging to someone else

3. *I sat in the third row at the concert.* What other meaning does *row* have?
Ⓐ an airplane
Ⓑ a goat
Ⓒ a way to move a boat
Ⓓ to play an instrument

4. *I dash out the door when I am late.* What other meaning does *dash* have?
Ⓐ walk slowly
Ⓑ skip
Ⓒ a sentence
Ⓓ a punctuation mark

5. *We need light to see.* What other meaning does *light* have?
Ⓐ very heavy
Ⓑ not heavy
Ⓒ easy to see
Ⓓ needed for sight

6. *I did not mean to upset you.* What other meaning does *mean* have?
Ⓐ upset
Ⓑ understanding
Ⓒ unkind
Ⓓ untidy

7. *Autumn is my favorite season.* What other meaning does *season* have?
Ⓐ to add spices
Ⓑ to eat
Ⓒ to cook
Ⓓ to order

8. *I like to play in my yard.* What other meaning does *yard* have?
Ⓐ parking lot
Ⓑ field
Ⓒ a standard measurement
Ⓓ a measuring tool

9. *I put the eraser at the tip of my pencil.* What other meaning does *tip* have?
Ⓐ to bake
Ⓑ to cover
Ⓒ to push over
Ⓓ to fill with water

10. *I hit the ball with the bat.* What other meaning does *bat* have?
Ⓐ an animal
Ⓑ an adventure
Ⓒ a mountain
Ⓓ a boot

Homophones

Fill in the blank with the best answer.

1. Please come over _____.
- Ⓐ hear
- Ⓑ here
- Ⓒ heer
- Ⓓ none of the above

2. I feel like I have a _____ in my stomach.
- Ⓐ knot
- Ⓑ not
- Ⓒ note
- Ⓓ none of the above

3. I would like you to meet my _____.
- Ⓐ ant
- Ⓑ annt
- Ⓒ aunt
- Ⓓ none of the above

4. The twins make a great _____.
- Ⓐ pare
- Ⓑ pear
- Ⓒ pair
- Ⓓ none of the above

5. Please be home by _____ o'clock.
- Ⓐ ate
- Ⓑ eight
- Ⓒ ayte
- Ⓓ none of the above

6. I wish you could come with us _____.
- Ⓐ to
- Ⓑ two
- Ⓒ too
- Ⓓ none of the above

7. I smell the _____ of chocolate.
- Ⓐ cent
- Ⓑ sent
- Ⓒ scent
- Ⓓ none of the above

8. The _____ ran away when it saw people.
- Ⓐ dear
- Ⓑ dere
- Ⓒ deer
- Ⓓ none of the above

9. I have an itch on the tip of my _____.
- Ⓐ knows
- Ⓑ nose
- Ⓒ knose
- Ⓓ none of the above

10. I can only play for an _____.
- Ⓐ ower
- Ⓑ our
- Ⓒ hour
- Ⓓ none of the above

Spelling

Answer the questions below.

1. Which word is misspelled?
   A sign
   B sing
   C salt
   D sange

2. What is the correct way to spell the number 12?
   A twelv
   B twelve
   C tweelv
   D towelv

3. Which word is spelled correctly?
   A intrest
   B flamme
   C trust
   D woodin

4. Which word is the correct spelling of a kind of car?
   A vann
   B van
   C truk
   D turuk

5. Which word is misspelled?
   A misstake
   B error
   C problem
   D issue

6. Which word is spelled correctly?
   A moniter
   B computor
   C keybord
   D mouse

7. Which month of the year is misspelled?
   A January
   B Febuary
   C November
   D December

8. Which type of food is misspelled?
   A hamburger
   B pretzel
   C samwich
   D soup

9. Which kind of storm is misspelled?
   A hurricane
   B tornado
   C thunderstorm
   D tyfoon

10. Which word is spelled correctly?
   A stream
   B forrest
   C leafs
   D soyl

Vocabulary

Choose the word that tells the meaning of each underlined word.

1. reasonable price
  Ⓐ fair
  Ⓑ smart
  Ⓒ forgetful
  Ⓓ expensive

2. overdue book
  Ⓐ good
  Ⓑ boring
  Ⓒ late
  Ⓓ special

3. tardy to school
  Ⓐ early
  Ⓑ happy
  Ⓒ worried
  Ⓓ late

4. outrageous lies
  Ⓐ wild
  Ⓑ funny
  Ⓒ tasty
  Ⓓ great

5. delicious snacks
  Ⓐ great smelling
  Ⓑ great looking
  Ⓒ great tasting
  Ⓓ great sounding

6. blaring siren
  Ⓐ loud
  Ⓑ colorful
  Ⓒ long
  Ⓓ empty

7. first-rate performance
  Ⓐ early
  Ⓑ on-time
  Ⓒ worst
  Ⓓ best

8. unexpected event
  Ⓐ unhappy
  Ⓑ surprising
  Ⓒ exciting
  Ⓓ holiday

9. favorite possession
  Ⓐ group
  Ⓑ money
  Ⓒ backpack
  Ⓓ belonging

10. happy clan
  Ⓐ class
  Ⓑ fish
  Ⓒ family
  Ⓓ ants

Context Clues

Find the meaning of each underlined word.

1. The fence was a <u>barrier</u> that kept the dog in our yard.
   - Ⓐ a dog
   - Ⓑ something that blocks the way
   - Ⓒ something that dogs need
   - Ⓓ a yard

2. My dad, the most <u>heroic</u> man I know, ran back into the fire to save our pet fish.
   - Ⓐ man
   - Ⓑ dad
   - Ⓒ brave
   - Ⓓ sad

3. It took us all day and tons of sand to build the <u>colossal</u> sand castle.
   - Ⓐ tiny
   - Ⓑ wet
   - Ⓒ creative
   - Ⓓ huge

4. I couldn't move in the backseat of the car because it was so <u>cramped</u>.
   - Ⓐ moving
   - Ⓑ crowded
   - Ⓒ ugly
   - Ⓓ big

5. After running six miles, Mom was <u>weary</u> and wanted to go home.
   - Ⓐ sick
   - Ⓑ perfect
   - Ⓒ happy
   - Ⓓ tired

6. His Invisible Man costume won a prize for being the most <u>unusual</u>.
   - Ⓐ original
   - Ⓑ scary
   - Ⓒ funny
   - Ⓓ expensive

7. The rain and clouds made it seem like a very <u>dreary</u> day.
   - Ⓐ sunny
   - Ⓑ gloomy
   - Ⓒ cold
   - Ⓓ hot

8. The island had water <u>surrounding</u> it.
   - Ⓐ on top
   - Ⓑ on one side
   - Ⓒ on two sides
   - Ⓓ on all sides

9. Get ready to leave, because the ship will <u>launch</u> from the dock at 3:00.
   - Ⓐ swim
   - Ⓑ take off
   - Ⓒ race
   - Ⓓ sink

10. My grandmother <u>mended</u> the socks so that I could wear them again.
   - Ⓐ sewed
   - Ⓑ ripped
   - Ⓒ threw out
   - Ⓓ bought new

Pronouns

Answer the questions below.

1. *Jeff and Lynn are late for school.* What pronoun describes *Jeff* and *Lynn*?
Ⓐ Them
Ⓑ They
Ⓒ She
Ⓓ He

2. *Jeff and Lynn are late for school.* What pronoun describes *school*?
Ⓐ them
Ⓑ they
Ⓒ it
Ⓓ that

3. *My class is going to put on a play.* What pronoun describes *my class*?
Ⓐ Us
Ⓑ They
Ⓒ We
Ⓓ It

4. *My class is going to put on a play.* How can the sentence be rewritten with a pronoun?
Ⓐ My class is going to play.
Ⓑ My class is going to put on them.
Ⓒ My class is going to put it on.
Ⓓ My class is going to play it on.

5. *I want to talk to Jo. How can I talk to her?* Who does the pronoun *her* refer to?
Ⓐ Jo
Ⓑ the author
Ⓒ Jo and the author
Ⓓ neither Jo nor the author

6. *My mother is my friend.* Who does the pronoun *my* refer to?
Ⓐ mother
Ⓑ the author
Ⓒ the author and mother
Ⓓ neither the author nor the mother

7. *Doug left his coat on the bench.* How can the sentence be rewritten with pronouns?
Ⓐ He left him on it.
Ⓑ Doug left it on he.
Ⓒ Doug left his coat it.
Ⓓ He left it there.

8. *My brother has to make his bed.* What pronoun can replace *my brother*?
Ⓐ Him
Ⓑ Her
Ⓒ He
Ⓓ It

9. *Let's turn at the next light.* How can the sentence be rewritten with a pronoun?
Ⓐ I turn at the next light.
Ⓑ We turn at the it.
Ⓒ Let's turn there.
Ⓓ Let's turn at that it.

10. *When can the baby and I play?* What pronoun can replace *the baby and I*?
Ⓐ us
Ⓑ we
Ⓒ me
Ⓓ she

Parts of Speech

Answer the questions below.

1. What part of speech is *river?*
  Ⓐ noun
  Ⓑ verb
  Ⓒ adjective
  Ⓓ preposition

2. What part of speech is *are?*
  Ⓐ noun
  Ⓑ verb
  Ⓒ adjective
  Ⓓ preposition

3. What part of speech is *on?*
  Ⓐ noun
  Ⓑ verb
  Ⓒ adjective
  Ⓓ preposition

4. What part of speech is *scary?*
  Ⓐ noun
  Ⓑ verb
  Ⓒ adjective
  Ⓓ preposition

5. What part of speech is *superior?*
  Ⓐ noun
  Ⓑ verb
  Ⓒ adjective
  Ⓓ preposition

6. What part of speech is *beneath?*
  Ⓐ noun
  Ⓑ verb
  Ⓒ adjective
  Ⓓ preposition

7. What is the adverb in the sentence below?
  He walked quietly down the street.
  Ⓐ walked
  Ⓑ quietly
  Ⓒ down
  Ⓓ street

8. What is the preposition in the sentence below?
  The car drove over the bridge.
  Ⓐ drove
  Ⓑ over
  Ⓒ the
  Ⓓ bridge

9. What is the article in the sentence below?
  The cat sat there.
  Ⓐ The
  Ⓑ cat
  Ⓒ sat
  Ⓓ there

10. What is the noun in the sentence below?
  Jane walked faster and faster.
  Ⓐ Jane
  Ⓑ walked
  Ⓒ faster
  Ⓓ and

Verb Tense

Answer the questions below.

1. What is the past tense of *agree?*
   - Ⓐ will agree
   - Ⓑ agreeing
   - Ⓒ agreed
   - Ⓓ agreement

2. What is the future tense of *come?*
   - Ⓐ coming
   - Ⓑ came
   - Ⓒ want to come
   - Ⓓ will come

3. What is the present tense of *saw?*
   - Ⓐ seed
   - Ⓑ see
   - Ⓒ sawed
   - Ⓓ will see

4. What is the past tense of *include?*
   - Ⓐ will include
   - Ⓑ includest
   - Ⓒ includeed
   - Ⓓ included

5. Which sentence is written in the past tense?
   - Ⓐ I just filled my backpack.
   - Ⓑ I will pack my bag for school.
   - Ⓒ When can I pack my backpack?
   - Ⓓ I am packing my bag for school.

6. Which sentence is written in the future tense?
   - Ⓐ Where did you come from?
   - Ⓑ Where will we be going?
   - Ⓒ Where are you going?
   - Ⓓ Where were you?

7. Which sentence is written in the present tense?
   - Ⓐ I will not be at the store.
   - Ⓑ I will be at the store.
   - Ⓒ I am at the store.
   - Ⓓ I was at the store.

8. Which sentence is **not** written in the present tense?
   - Ⓐ Can I help you?
   - Ⓑ I am happy to see you.
   - Ⓒ I was here first.
   - Ⓓ I like popcorn and apples.

9. Which sentence is **not** written in the future tense?
   - Ⓐ I was late for school.
   - Ⓑ I will finish my dinner.
   - Ⓒ I will be going to soccer practice.
   - Ⓓ I will go to the park now.

10. Which sentence is **not** written in the past tense?
    - Ⓐ Julia saw the movie first.
    - Ⓑ Dominick saw the movie second.
    - Ⓒ Alec saw the movie last night.
    - Ⓓ Ben will see the movie tomorrow.

Subject and Verb Agreement

Answer the questions below.

1. Which sentence is written correctly?
Ⓐ She want a glass of milk.
Ⓑ She wants a glass of milk.
Ⓒ She wanting a glass of milk.
Ⓓ She want milk glass.

2. Which sentence is written correctly?
Ⓐ The three bears goed for a walk.
Ⓑ The three bears will goed for a walk.
Ⓒ The three bears to go for a walk.
Ⓓ The three bears go for a walk.

3. Which verb correctly completes the sentence below?
After three years, she _____ new boots.
Ⓐ buy
Ⓑ buying
Ⓒ bought
Ⓓ buyed

4. Which verb correctly completes the sentence below?
Bill _____ to find his keys.
Ⓐ tries
Ⓑ try
Ⓒ trying
Ⓓ will tries

5. Which sentence is written correctly?
Ⓐ This are my favorite books.
Ⓑ These is my favorite books.
Ⓒ These are my favorite books.
Ⓓ This is my favorite books.

6. Which sentence is written correctly?
Ⓐ He wishes for a snow day.
Ⓑ We wishes for a snow day.
Ⓒ They wishes for a snow day.
Ⓓ I wishes for a snow day.

7. Which sentence is written correctly?
Ⓐ I like spaghetti and meatballs.
Ⓑ I likes spaghetti and meatballs.
Ⓒ He like spaghetti and meatballs.
Ⓓ They likes spaghetti and meatballs.

8. Which subject correctly completes the sentence below?
_____ eats the carrots.
Ⓐ We
Ⓑ The rabbit
Ⓒ They
Ⓓ I

9. Which subject correctly completes the sentence below?
_____ meets with her teacher after school.
Ⓐ I
Ⓑ They
Ⓒ We
Ⓓ She

10. Which subject correctly completes the sentence below?
_____ think they might be late.
Ⓐ Joseph
Ⓑ Allen
Ⓒ Joseph and Allen
Ⓓ He

Irregular Verbs

Choose the past tense of each verb.

1. catch
Ⓐ catched
Ⓑ caught
Ⓒ catch
Ⓓ catches

2. keep
Ⓐ kept
Ⓑ keeped
Ⓒ kepted
Ⓓ keep

3. come
Ⓐ comed
Ⓑ comes
Ⓒ camed
Ⓓ came

4. make
Ⓐ maker
Ⓑ makes
Ⓒ made
Ⓓ maked

5. drink
Ⓐ drank
Ⓑ dranked
Ⓒ drinked
Ⓓ drink

6. sleep
Ⓐ sleeped
Ⓑ sleepd
Ⓒ slepted
Ⓓ slept

7. be
Ⓐ was
Ⓑ were
Ⓒ been
Ⓓ all of the above

8. say
Ⓐ sayed
Ⓑ said
Ⓒ saw
Ⓓ sawed

9. see
Ⓐ saw
Ⓑ sawed
Ⓒ seed
Ⓓ seen

10. tell
Ⓐ telld
Ⓑ telled
Ⓒ told
Ⓓ tolded

Editing and Proofreading

Answer the questions below.

1. How can the sentence below be corrected?

The dog goed to the store with its owner.

Ⓐ The dog goed to the stores with its owner.

Ⓑ The dog goed to the store with its owners.

Ⓒ The dog went to the store with its owner.

Ⓓ The dog went to the store withs its owners.

2. How can the sentence below be corrected?

I can't make it to the party on July 12 2009.

Ⓐ I can't makes it to the party on July 12 2009.

Ⓑ I can'ts makes it to the party on July 12 2009.

Ⓒ I can't make it to the party on July 12, 2009.

Ⓓ I can't make it to the party on July, 12 2009.

3. How can the sentence below be corrected?

The spider spinned the web quick.

Ⓐ The spider quickly spun the web.

Ⓑ The spider spinnd the web quick.

Ⓒ The spider spunned the web quickly.

Ⓓ The spider quickly spin the web.

4. How can the sentence below be corrected?

Why should I say that.

Ⓐ Why should I say that?

Ⓑ Why should I says that?

Ⓒ Why should I said that?

Ⓓ Why shoulds I says that?

5. How can the sentence below be corrected?

We can't wait to see you on labor day.

Ⓐ We can't waits to sees you on labor day.

Ⓑ We can't waits to see you on labor day.

Ⓒ We can't wait to sees you on Labor Day.

Ⓓ We can't wait to see you on Labor Day.

6. How can the sentence below be corrected?

We loved our dogs but it ran away.

Ⓐ We loved our dogs but theys ran away.

Ⓑ We loved our dog but it ran away.

Ⓒ We loved our dog but it rans away.

Ⓓ We loved our dog but they ran away.

Section 3: Test

Read the passages and answer the questions.

Sara's Big Day

Sara is ready for her first babysitting job. She has grown up next door to the Marsh family her whole life. She visited the hospital when baby Marco was born five years ago. Sara is a smart and responsible girl and Marco likes her a lot. While Marco's mother goes to the store this afternoon, Sara will go and watch Marco. Mrs. Marsh will only be gone about an hour. Sara also agreed to stay in the house with Marco while his mother puts the groceries away. If everything goes well, Sara might be able to watch Marco again. She will be an official babysitter. She cannot wait!

1. Who is the main character in the story?
Ⓐ Marco
Ⓑ Marco's mother
Ⓒ Sara
Ⓓ Sara's mother

2. How would you describe Sara?
Ⓐ impatient
Ⓑ reliable
Ⓒ bored
Ⓓ mean

3. What is the main idea of the story?
Ⓐ Sara visited Marco in the hospital when he was born.
Ⓑ Sara will babysit Marco when Mrs. Marsh puts away the groceries.
Ⓒ Sara is about to babysit for the first time.
Ⓓ Marco likes Sara a lot.

4. What is another good title for this passage?
Ⓐ "Sara's First Babysitting Job"
Ⓑ "Marco's Favorite Babysitter"
Ⓒ "Sara and Marco's Day at the Zoo"
Ⓓ "Mrs. Marsh Goes to the Store"

5. From the context of the story, what does the word *official* mean?
Ⓐ real
Ⓑ happy
Ⓒ good
Ⓓ young

6. How do you think Sara feels about her first babysitting job?
Ⓐ scared
Ⓑ angry
Ⓒ nervous
Ⓓ excited

Tsunami!

Have you ever been to the beach? Do you remember the ocean waves? They can be gentle and calm. They can also be large and violent. A tsunami is a series of huge waves that suddenly washes over the land. A tsunami can happen after underwater movements, such as earthquakes or volcanic eruptions.

Right before a tsunami hits, about half the water on a beach will look like it has disappeared. The water rushes out to the sea to give the waves more energy before they head back to the shore. Suddenly, tall powerful waves hit and take over the land. Nothing can stop a tsunami. The best thing to do is get far away from the beach if you know an earthquake just happened at sea.

7. Which is the most important supporting detail?
   Ⓐ Many people have seen waves.
   Ⓑ Waves can be gentle and calm.
   Ⓒ Nothing can stop a tsunami.
   Ⓓ A tsunami can happen after large underwater movements.

8. What is the **most likely** effect of a tsunami?
   Ⓐ damage to land
   Ⓑ dry land
   Ⓒ earthquakes
   Ⓓ volcanic eruptions

9. Is the passage mainly fact or opinion?
   Ⓐ fact
   Ⓑ opinion
   Ⓒ neither fact or opinion
   Ⓓ equally fact and opinion

10. How many paragraphs are in the passage?
    Ⓐ 1
    Ⓑ 2
    Ⓒ 3
    Ⓓ 4

11. What is the author's purpose for writing the passage?
    Ⓐ to entertain the reader about disasters
    Ⓑ to inform the reader about tsunamis and how they are caused
    Ⓒ to persuade the reader to learn more about tsunamis
    Ⓓ to persuade the reader to try to stop tsunamis

12. Why might someone want to get out of the way of a tsunami?
    Ⓐ They are very annoying.
    Ⓑ They are very dangerous.
    Ⓒ They hit the shore very slowly.
    Ⓓ They are not very powerful.

13. Which sentence is written correctly?
Ⓐ We walked through the Park, and ate lunch.
Ⓑ They wants to tell us what to say.
Ⓒ Caleb was sleeping through his Birthday Party.
Ⓓ After Columbus Day we had to start raking leaves.

14. Which word uses the prefix that means *not?*
Ⓐ preview
Ⓑ reinvent
Ⓒ unclean
Ⓓ extraordinary

15. Which word uses the suffix that means *a person who?*
Ⓐ dentistry
Ⓑ cleaning
Ⓒ baker
Ⓓ invitation

16. Which word has a long *u* sound?
Ⓐ plate
Ⓑ put
Ⓒ great
Ⓓ cute

17. Which sentence does **not** show subject and verb agreement?
Ⓐ We can tell them what we think.
Ⓑ They helps us with our homework.
Ⓒ Mr. Lee watched his favorite movie.
Ⓓ My teacher knows I can play the flute.

18. *Tommy and Raj were late for the soccer game.* Which shows the sentence rewritten with pronouns?
Ⓐ Tommy and Raj were late for them.
Ⓑ Tommy and Raj were late for us.
Ⓒ They were late for it.
Ⓓ They were late for the games.

19. Which word has more than one meaning?
Ⓐ chair
Ⓑ dirt
Ⓒ bat
Ⓓ under

20. Which word is a compound word?
Ⓐ hammer
Ⓑ flying
Ⓒ shopper
Ⓓ nightfall

21. Which word is an antonym for *create?*
Ⓐ explain
Ⓑ destroy
Ⓒ make
Ⓓ try

22. Which word is a synonym for *scream?*
Ⓐ yell
Ⓑ whisper
Ⓒ speak
Ⓓ sing

23. Which word shows the past tense of *forget?*
Ⓐ forgot
Ⓑ forgotted
Ⓒ forgetted
Ⓓ forgets

24. Which word sounds like *need?*
Ⓐ nead
Ⓑ nede
Ⓒ knead
Ⓓ kneed

25. *My mother was furious when she saw my messy room.* What does *furious* mean?
Ⓐ helpful
Ⓑ happy
Ⓒ angry
Ⓓ sad

26. Which word has a short vowel sound?
Ⓐ light
Ⓑ came
Ⓒ tried
Ⓓ stuck

27. Which sentence is written correctly?
Ⓐ Their father saws how happy they was with the toys.
Ⓑ Their father saw how happy they were with the toys.
Ⓒ Their father sees how happy they were with the toys.
Ⓓ Their father saw how happy they was with the toys.

28. Which sentence is written in the present tense?
Ⓐ We will try to return the books on time.
Ⓑ We did not want to stay late at the party.
Ⓒ We cannot tell what the sign says.
Ⓓ We wanted to tell you what happened after school.

29. What is the past tense of *buy?*
Ⓐ buyed
Ⓑ bought
Ⓒ boughted
Ⓓ buyd

30. Which shows the present tense?
Ⓐ When will we make a snowman?
Ⓑ I will rake the leaves.
Ⓒ I went swimming.
Ⓓ We are looking at the flowers.

31. Which shows the correct punctuation?
Ⓐ Are you going to help me.
Ⓑ When are we going!
Ⓒ My mom will pick you up at 300 PM.
Ⓓ Your sister has a dance class in an hour.

32. Which shows the correct capitalization?
Ⓐ Monica and sonal want to carry the bags.
Ⓑ The fourth of July is my favorite holiday.
Ⓒ We cannot play in Lincoln Park until this afternoon.
Ⓓ let me walk you to Main Street.

Unit 2

Section 4: Number Sense
Place Value

Answer the questions below.

1. What is the value of the 7 in 7,629?

- Ⓐ 7
- Ⓑ 70
- Ⓒ 700
- Ⓓ 7,000

2. In what place value is the 0 in 33,102?

- Ⓐ ones
- Ⓑ tens
- Ⓒ hundreds
- Ⓓ thousands

3. What is the value of the 1 in 1,023?

- Ⓐ one thousand
- Ⓑ one hundred
- Ⓒ ten
- Ⓓ one

4. What is the value of the 9 in 2,359?

- Ⓐ 9,000
- Ⓑ 900
- Ⓒ 90
- Ⓓ 9

5. How many hundreds are in 3,021?

- Ⓐ 0
- Ⓑ 1
- Ⓒ 2
- Ⓓ 3

6. Which number shows two hundred five?

- Ⓐ 250
- Ⓑ 215
- Ⓒ 205
- Ⓓ 200

7. Which number has 8 thousands, 3 hundreds, 2 tens, and 4 ones?

- Ⓐ 8,342
- Ⓑ 8,324
- Ⓒ 8,234
- Ⓓ 4,238

8. What is the value of the 5 in 1,352?

- Ⓐ 5,000
- Ⓑ 500
- Ⓒ 50
- Ⓓ 5

9. What is the value of the 1 in 2,910?

- Ⓐ 1,000
- Ⓑ 100
- Ⓒ 10
- Ⓓ 1

10. Which number shows twenty-three thousand and eight?

- Ⓐ 8
- Ⓑ 23,800
- Ⓒ 23,080
- Ⓓ 23,008

Comparing and Ordering Numbers

Answer the questions below.

1. Which number sentence is correct?
Ⓐ 785 < 685
Ⓑ 786 > 799
Ⓒ 322 > 3,222
Ⓓ 902 < 920

2. Which number has the greatest value?
Ⓐ 0
Ⓑ 34
Ⓒ 57
Ⓓ 91

3. Which shows the numbers in order from least to greatest?
Ⓐ 344, 322, 333, 311
Ⓑ 112, 133, 135, 136
Ⓒ 9,344, 9,422, 9,301, 9,156
Ⓓ 682, 673, 653, 601

4. Which number has the least value?
Ⓐ 38,033
Ⓑ 38,300
Ⓒ 38,303
Ⓓ 38,803

5. Which number sentence is correct?
Ⓐ 92 < 90
Ⓑ 45 > 47
Ⓒ 102 = 201
Ⓓ 65 > 56

6. Which number sentence is correct?
Ⓐ 37 > 49
Ⓑ 26 > 21
Ⓒ 97 < 77
Ⓓ 82 < 12

7. Which shows the numbers in order from greatest to least?
Ⓐ 96, 98, 100, 102
Ⓑ 83, 81, 79, 77
Ⓒ 32, 65, 92, 23
Ⓓ 83, 92, 81, 93

8. Choose the correct symbol to complete the number sentence.
82 _____ 28
Ⓐ >
Ⓑ <
Ⓒ =
Ⓓ none of the above

9. Choose the correct symbol to complete the number sentence.
97 _____ 56
Ⓐ >
Ⓑ <
Ⓒ =
Ⓓ none of the above

10. Choose the correct symbol to complete the number sentence.
20 _____ 45
Ⓐ >
Ⓑ <
Ⓒ =
Ⓓ none of the above

Adding and Subtracting Whole Numbers

Answer the questions below.

1. 84 + 9 =
Ⓐ 91
Ⓑ 93
Ⓒ 95
Ⓓ 134

2. 823 + 82 =
Ⓐ 895
Ⓑ 899
Ⓒ 905
Ⓓ 950

3. 782 + 26 =
Ⓐ 808
Ⓑ 708
Ⓒ 707
Ⓓ 609

4. 25 + 7 =
Ⓐ 36
Ⓑ 34
Ⓒ 32
Ⓓ 30

5. 50 + 30 =
Ⓐ 90
Ⓑ 80
Ⓒ 60
Ⓓ 20

6. 29 + 18 + 4 =
Ⓐ 51
Ⓑ 47
Ⓒ 33
Ⓓ 22

7. 75 − 23 =
Ⓐ 22
Ⓑ 34
Ⓒ 52
Ⓓ 50

8. 121 − 54 =
Ⓐ 57
Ⓑ 67
Ⓒ 60
Ⓓ 77

9. 93 − 56 =
Ⓐ 37
Ⓑ 30
Ⓒ 47
Ⓓ 45

10. 560 − 438 =
Ⓐ 22
Ⓑ 187
Ⓒ 233
Ⓓ 122

11. 200 − 55 − 25 =
Ⓐ 230
Ⓑ 225
Ⓒ 120
Ⓓ 200

12. 333 − 30 − 100 =
Ⓐ 203
Ⓑ 100
Ⓒ 200
Ⓓ 103

Multiplying and Dividing Whole Numbers

Answer the questions below.

1. $31 \times 4 =$
- (A) 112
- (B) 124
- (C) 134
- (D) 135

2. $53 \times 3 =$
- (A) 159
- (B) 161
- (C) 164
- (D) 169

3. $674 \times 2 =$
- (A) 1,318
- (B) 1,328
- (C) 1,348
- (D) 1,448

4. $832 \times 5 =$
- (A) 4,160
- (B) 4,060
- (C) 3,674
- (D) 3,328

5. $2,213 \times 2 =$
- (A) 4,462
- (B) 4,426
- (C) 4,246
- (D) 4,226

6. $3,069 \times 5 =$
- (A) 12,345
- (B) 5,500
- (C) 15,345
- (D) 14,305

7. $96 \div 3 =$
- (A) 29
- (B) 30
- (C) 31
- (D) 32

8. $49 \div 3 =$
- (A) 16
- (B) 16 R1
- (C) 16 R2
- (D) 17

9. $382 \div 4 =$
- (A) 95
- (B) 95 R1
- (C) 95 R2
- (D) 95 R3

10. $485 \div 5 =$
- (A) 97
- (B) 96
- (C) 96 R1
- (D) 95

11. $64 \div 8 =$
- (A) 9
- (B) 8 R1
- (C) 8
- (D) 7 R1

12. $387 \div 5 =$
- (A) 77 R1
- (B) 77 R2
- (C) 77 R3
- (D) 77

Adding and Subtracting Decimals

Answer the questions below.

1. 7.3 + 8.3 =
Ⓐ 14.6
Ⓑ 14.9
Ⓒ 15.6
Ⓓ 15.9

2. 1.9 + 3.4 =
Ⓐ 5.3
Ⓑ 5.4
Ⓒ 6.3
Ⓓ 6.4

3. 3.2 + 3.7 =
Ⓐ 6.8
Ⓑ 6.9
Ⓒ 7.1
Ⓓ 7.9

4. 56.3 + 43.8 =
Ⓐ 101.1
Ⓑ 100.1
Ⓒ 10.01
Ⓓ 10.1

5. 78.65 + 54.81 =
Ⓐ 13.46
Ⓑ 13.36
Ⓒ 133.36
Ⓓ 133.46

6. 68.51 + 73.33 =
Ⓐ 130.74
Ⓑ 131.84
Ⓒ 140.84
Ⓓ 141.84

7. 9.9 − 8.4 =
Ⓐ 11.5
Ⓑ 1.5
Ⓒ 1.4
Ⓓ 1.3

8. 82.3 − 75.3 =
Ⓐ 7.0
Ⓑ 7.3
Ⓒ 8.0
Ⓓ 8.3

9. 47.12 − 38.12 =
Ⓐ 9.12
Ⓑ 9.0
Ⓒ 8.12
Ⓓ 8.0

10. 86.23 − 23.55 =
Ⓐ 59.08
Ⓑ 59.18
Ⓒ 62.65
Ⓓ 62.68

11. 8.3 − 4.2 =
Ⓐ 41.1
Ⓑ 41
Ⓒ 4.1
Ⓓ 4.0

12. 98.65 − 64.75 =
Ⓐ 33.9
Ⓑ 34.9
Ⓒ 33.99
Ⓓ 30.9

Problems and Solutions

Answer the questions below.

1. Gustavo's class picked 108 apples on their class trip to the apple orchard. Bali's class picked 184 apples. How many apples did the classes pick in all?

Ⓐ 301
Ⓑ 292
Ⓒ 275
Ⓓ 262

2. Mrs. Kramer baked 382 brownies for the school bake sale. She sold 297 of them. How many brownies did she have left?

Ⓐ 85
Ⓑ 84
Ⓒ 77
Ⓓ 75

3. Minnie gave 3 apples to each of her 17 classmates. How many apples did Minnie give out in all?

Ⓐ 17
Ⓑ 20
Ⓒ 49
Ⓓ 51

4. Logan has 72 baseball cards. He put the cards into 8 piles. How many cards are in each pile?

Ⓐ 10
Ⓑ 9
Ⓒ 8
Ⓓ 7

5. Sloan ate 27 chocolate candies on Monday, Tuesday, and Wednesday. How many chocolate candies did she eat in all?

Ⓐ 78
Ⓑ 79
Ⓒ 80
Ⓓ 81

6. Mr. Diaz ordered 96 books for the classroom library. He divided the books equally among 12 bookshelves. How many books are on each shelf?

Ⓐ 6
Ⓑ 7
Ⓒ 8
Ⓓ 9

Word Problems with Money

Answer the questions below.

1. Keisha bought a stuffed dog for $5.30 and an umbrella for $12.50. How much did Keisha spend in all?
- Ⓐ $18.00
- Ⓑ $17.80
- Ⓒ $17.70
- Ⓓ $15.40

2. Mr. Anders has $10. He buys a movie ticket for $7.50. How much money does he have left?
- Ⓐ $2.50
- Ⓑ $2.75
- Ⓒ $3.50
- Ⓓ $3.75

3. Manny bought 4 books for $4.25 each. How much did he spend in all?
- Ⓐ $17.75
- Ⓑ $17.50
- Ⓒ $17.25
- Ⓓ $17.00

4. Abby has $20. She gives $5 to each of her sisters and has no money left. How many sisters does Abby have?
- Ⓐ 2
- Ⓑ 3
- Ⓒ 4
- Ⓓ 5

5. Tony earned $15.75 by mowing lawns. How much more does he have to earn to have $20?
- Ⓐ $4.50
- Ⓑ $3.75
- Ⓒ $4.00
- Ⓓ $4.25

6. Grandpa spent $10.50 on each of his 5 grandchildren. How much money did he spend?
- Ⓐ $51
- Ⓑ $50.50
- Ⓒ $52.50
- Ⓓ $50

Fractions

Answer the questions below.

1. Which fraction is largest?

Ⓐ $\frac{1}{2}$

Ⓑ $\frac{1}{4}$

Ⓒ $\frac{1}{3}$

Ⓓ $\frac{1}{5}$

2. Which fraction is smallest?

Ⓐ $\frac{3}{4}$

Ⓑ $\frac{2}{3}$

Ⓒ $\frac{4}{5}$

Ⓓ $\frac{3}{5}$

3. $\frac{1}{5} + \frac{3}{5} =$

Ⓐ $\frac{1}{5}$

Ⓑ $\frac{2}{5}$

Ⓒ $\frac{4}{5}$

Ⓓ $\frac{5}{5}$

4. $\frac{3}{8} - \frac{2}{8} =$

Ⓐ $\frac{1}{8}$

Ⓑ $\frac{2}{8}$

Ⓒ $\frac{3}{8}$

Ⓓ $\frac{4}{8}$

5. What fraction does the picture show?

Ⓐ $\frac{2}{3}$

Ⓑ $\frac{3}{5}$

Ⓒ $\frac{2}{4}$

Ⓓ $\frac{2}{6}$

6. What fraction does the picture show?

Ⓐ $\frac{1}{8}$

Ⓑ $\frac{2}{6}$

Ⓒ $\frac{2}{8}$

Ⓓ $\frac{3}{8}$

7. Which number sentence shows $\frac{1}{5}$?

Ⓐ $\frac{4}{5} - \frac{2}{5}$

Ⓑ $\frac{3}{5} - \frac{1}{5}$

Ⓒ $\frac{5}{5} - \frac{2}{5}$

Ⓓ $\frac{4}{5} - \frac{3}{5}$

8. Which number sentence shows $\frac{2}{3}$?

Ⓐ $\frac{3}{6} + \frac{3}{6}$

Ⓑ $\frac{3}{6} + \frac{2}{6}$

Ⓒ $\frac{2}{6} + \frac{2}{6}$

Ⓓ $\frac{1}{6} + \frac{5}{6}$

9. Which fraction equals 1?

Ⓐ $\frac{1}{4}$

Ⓑ $\frac{2}{4}$

Ⓒ $\frac{3}{4}$

Ⓓ $\frac{4}{4}$

10. Which fraction equals 0?

Ⓐ $\frac{0}{3}$

Ⓑ $\frac{1}{3}$

Ⓒ $\frac{2}{3}$

Ⓓ $\frac{3}{3}$

Section 5: Algebra and Functions
Number Patterns

Answer the questions below.

1. What is the missing number in the pattern?

70, 80, 90, _____, 110, 120

Ⓐ 99
Ⓑ 100
Ⓒ 101
Ⓓ 110

2. What is the rule of this number pattern?

2; 20; 200; 2,000; 20,000; 200,000

Ⓐ multiply by 2
Ⓑ multiply by 20
Ⓒ multiply by 10
Ⓓ multiply by 100

3. What are the next three numbers in this pattern?

6, 12, 18, 24, 30, _____, _____, _____

Ⓐ 36, 46, 56
Ⓑ 36, 42, 52
Ⓒ 36, 42, 48
Ⓓ 38, 42, 58

4. What is the number that is missing in the pattern?

1,222, 1,223, 1,224, _____, 1,226

Ⓐ 1,227
Ⓑ 1,225
Ⓒ 1,220
Ⓓ 124

5. What is the next number in the pattern?

600, 700, 800, 900, _____

Ⓐ 1,999
Ⓑ 1,000
Ⓒ 100
Ⓓ 10

6. Which number sentence fits into the pattern?

70 + 1, 70 + 2, 70 + 3, 70 + 4, _____

Ⓐ 75 + 1
Ⓑ 75 + 5
Ⓒ 70 + 1
Ⓓ 70 + 5

7. What is the rule of this number pattern?

8, 11, 14, 17, 20, 23, 26

Ⓐ multiply by 2
Ⓑ multiply by 3
Ⓒ add 2
Ⓓ add 3

8. What is the rule of this number pattern?

1, 5, 9, 13, 17, 21, 25, 29

Ⓐ multiply by 1
Ⓑ add 3
Ⓒ add 4
Ⓓ There is no pattern.

Choosing the Operation

Choose the operation that completes each number sentence.

1. 5 ___ 9 = 45
- Ⓐ +
- Ⓑ −
- Ⓒ ×
- Ⓓ ÷

2. 731 ___ 258 = 989
- Ⓐ +
- Ⓑ −
- Ⓒ ×
- Ⓓ ÷

3. 45 ___ 32 = 13
- Ⓐ +
- Ⓑ −
- Ⓒ ×
- Ⓓ ÷

4. 84 ___ 7 = 12
- Ⓐ +
- Ⓑ −
- Ⓒ ×
- Ⓓ ÷

5. 7 ___ 9 = 63
- Ⓐ +
- Ⓑ −
- Ⓒ ×
- Ⓓ ÷

6. 322 ___ 42 = 364
- Ⓐ +
- Ⓑ −
- Ⓒ ×
- Ⓓ ÷

7. 73 ___ 24 = 49
- Ⓐ +
- Ⓑ −
- Ⓒ ×
- Ⓓ ÷

8. 321 ___ 3 = 107
- Ⓐ +
- Ⓑ −
- Ⓒ ×
- Ⓓ ÷

9. 52 ___ 3 = 156
- Ⓐ +
- Ⓑ −
- Ⓒ ×
- Ⓓ ÷

10. 467 ___ 199 = 268
- Ⓐ +
- Ⓑ −
- Ⓒ ×
- Ⓓ ÷

Properties of Addition and Subtraction

Choose the property that each number sentence shows.

1. $45 + 0 = 45$
  Ⓐ Commutative Property
  Ⓑ Associative Property
  Ⓒ Distributive Property
  Ⓓ Identity Property

2. $(15 + 2) + 6 = 15 + (2 + 6)$
  Ⓐ Commutative Property
  Ⓑ Associative Property
  Ⓒ Distributive Property
  Ⓓ Identity Property

3. $34 + 81 = 81 + 34$
  Ⓐ Commutative Property
  Ⓑ Associative Property
  Ⓒ Distributive Property
  Ⓓ Identity Property

4. $2 \times (3 + 5) = (2 \times 3) + (2 \times 5)$
  Ⓐ Commutative Property
  Ⓑ Associative Property
  Ⓒ Distributive Property
  Ⓓ Identity Property

5. $73 - 0 = 73$
  Ⓐ Commutative Property
  Ⓑ Associative Property
  Ⓒ Distributive Property
  Ⓓ Identity Property

6. $7 \times (5 - 2) = (7 \times 5) - (7 \times 2)$
  Ⓐ Commutative Property
  Ⓑ Associative Property
  Ⓒ Distributive Property
  Ⓓ Identity Property

7. $8 + 21 = 21 + 8$
  Ⓐ Commutative Property
  Ⓑ Associative Property
  Ⓒ Distributive Property
  Ⓓ Identity Property

8. $4 + (2 - 1) = (4 + 2) - (4 - 3)$
  Ⓐ Commutative Property
  Ⓑ Associative Property
  Ⓒ Distributive Property
  Ⓓ Identity Property

9. $0 - 0 = 0$
  Ⓐ Commutative Property
  Ⓑ Associative Property
  Ⓒ Distributive Property
  Ⓓ Identity Property

10. $(5 + 7) + 10 = 5 + (7 + 10)$
  Ⓐ Commutative Property
  Ⓑ Associative Property
  Ⓒ Distributive Property
  Ⓓ Identity Property

Properties of Multiplication and Division

Answer the questions below.

1. Which number sentence shows the Commutative Property of Multiplication?
   Ⓐ $8 \times 3 = 8 + 3$
   Ⓑ $14 \times 3 = 3 \times 14$
   Ⓒ $14 \times 1 = 14$
   Ⓓ $14 \times 0 = 0$

2. Which number sentence shows the Identity Property of Division?
   Ⓐ $9 \div 1 = 9$
   Ⓑ $9 \div 9 = 1$
   Ⓒ $9 \div 0 = 0$
   Ⓓ $9 \div 9 = 0$

3. Which number sentence shows the Associative Property of Multiplication?
   Ⓐ $8 \times (3 \times 4) = (8 \times 3) \times 4$
   Ⓑ $8 - (4 \times 1) = 1 \times (4 \times 8)$
   Ⓒ $7 + (2 \times 4) = 2 + (7 \times 4)$
   Ⓓ $9 + (6 \div 2) = 2 + (9 \div 6)$

4. Which number sentence shows the Distributive Property of Multiplication?
   Ⓐ $3 \times (2 + 4) = 3 \times 2 \times 4$
   Ⓑ $3 \times (2 + 4) = (3 \times 2) \times (3 \times 4)$
   Ⓒ $3 \times (2 + 4) = (3 \times 2) + (3 \times 4)$
   Ⓓ $3 \times (2 + 4) = (3 + 2) + (3 \times 4)$

5. $42 \div 1 =$
   Ⓐ 42
   Ⓑ 12
   Ⓒ 1
   Ⓓ 0

6. $8 \times 3 =$
   Ⓐ $3 + 8$
   Ⓑ 3×8
   Ⓒ $8 - 3$
   Ⓓ $8 \div 3$

7. $(2 \times 7) \times 4 =$
   Ⓐ $(2 \times 7) + 4$
   Ⓑ $(2 + 7) + 4$
   Ⓒ $2 \times (7 \times 4)$
   Ⓓ $2 + (7 \times 4)$

8. $0 \times 4 =$
   Ⓐ 0
   Ⓑ 1
   Ⓒ 4
   Ⓓ 8

9. $7 \times (2 + 8) =$
   Ⓐ $2 \times (7 + 8)$
   Ⓑ $7 + (2 \times 8)$
   Ⓒ $(7 + 2) \times (7 + 8)$
   Ⓓ $(7 \times 2) + (7 \times 8)$

10. $7 \times 4 \times 9 =$
    Ⓐ 7×9
    Ⓑ $9 \times 4 \times 7$
    Ⓒ $9 \times 4 + 7$
    Ⓓ $4 + 7 + 9$

Functions

Use the function table to answer questions 1–4.

2	4	6	8	10
6	12	18	24	?

1. What is the rule of the function table?
  Ⓐ multiply by 2
  Ⓑ multiply by 3
  Ⓒ add 6
  Ⓓ add 8

2. What number sentence can be used to show the first column of the function table?
  Ⓐ $2 + 4 = 6$
  Ⓑ $2 \times 3 = 6$
  Ⓒ $2 + 6 = 8$
  Ⓓ $2 \times 6 = 12$

3. What is the value of the missing number in the function table?
  Ⓐ 40
  Ⓑ 35
  Ⓒ 30
  Ⓓ 25

4. Which column shows $8 \times$ ___ $= 24$?
  Ⓐ column 1
  Ⓑ column 2
  Ⓒ column 3
  Ⓓ column 4

Use the function table to answer questions 5–8.

5	10	15	20	25
10	20	?	40	50

5. What is the rule of the function table?
  Ⓐ add 5
  Ⓑ add 10
  Ⓒ multiply by 2
  Ⓓ multiply by 5

6. What is the value of the missing number in the function table?
  Ⓐ 25
  Ⓑ 30
  Ⓒ 35
  Ⓓ 40

7. What would the next column of the table be?
  Ⓐ 25 on the top, 50 on the bottom
  Ⓑ 30 on the top, 55 on the bottom
  Ⓒ 30 on the top, 60 on the bottom
  Ⓓ 40 on the top, 60 on the bottom

8. Which number sentence can be used to show the second column of the table?
  Ⓐ $10 + 10 = 20$
  Ⓑ $10 \times 10 = 20$
  Ⓒ $20 - 10 = 10$
  Ⓓ $10 \times 2 = 20$

Finding the Variable

Answer the questions below.

1. $9 \times \underline{} = 81$
(A) 9
(B) 8
(C) 7
(D) 6

2. $12 + \underline{} = 36$
(A) 3
(B) 6
(C) 12
(D) 24

3. $16 + \underline{} = 20$
(A) 2
(B) 4
(C) 6
(D) 8

4. $64 \div \underline{} = 4$
(A) 16
(B) 12
(C) 10
(D) 8

5. $72 \div \underline{} = 2$
(A) 42
(B) 38
(C) 36
(D) 32

6. $15 \times \underline{} = 90$
(A) 5
(B) 6
(C) 75
(D) 85

7. $112 - \underline{} = 86$
(A) 12
(B) 16
(C) 26
(D) 28

8. $77 - \underline{} = 55$
(A) 22
(B) 20
(C) 18
(D) 2

9. $\underline{} \times 14 = 42$
(A) 2
(B) 3
(C) 4
(D) 5

10. $\underline{} - 15 = 30$
(A) 0
(B) 1
(C) 30
(D) 45

Word Problems

Answer the questions below.

1. Deshaun's bus drives him 2 miles to school each morning. Which number sentence shows how many mornings it would take Deshaun's bus driver to travel 50 miles?
   Ⓐ $2 \times 50 = \underline{\hspace{1cm}}$
   Ⓑ $2 \div 50 = \underline{\hspace{1cm}}$
   Ⓒ $2 \times \underline{\hspace{0.7cm}} = 50$
   Ⓓ $50 \div \underline{\hspace{1cm}} = 5$

2. Marco talks to his grandmother on the phone for 20 minutes each day. How many days does it take Marco to talk to his grandmother for 120 minutes?
   Ⓐ 4
   Ⓑ 5
   Ⓒ 6
   Ⓓ 7

3. Laura's class is setting up the gymnasium for a school concert. Each row of seats has 16 chairs in it. Which number sentence shows the number of rows they will need to have if they want to set up 320 seats for the concert?
   Ⓐ $320 - 16 = \underline{\hspace{0.7cm}}$
   Ⓑ $320 - \underline{\hspace{0.7cm}} = 16$
   Ⓒ $16 \div \underline{\hspace{0.7cm}} = 320$
   Ⓓ $16 \times \underline{\hspace{0.7cm}} = 320$

4. Jonas raked 12 bags of leaves from his yard for 4 weekends in a row. Which operation is **best** to use to find out how many bags Jonas raked in all?
   Ⓐ addition
   Ⓑ subtraction
   Ⓒ multiplication
   Ⓓ division

5. Mrs. Mui baked 224 cookies for the bake sale. It took 7 hours to bake the cookies. How many cookies did Mrs. Mui bake per hour?
   Ⓐ 23
   Ⓑ 32
   Ⓒ 30
   Ⓓ 35

6. Deepak walks 1.6 miles to school every day. Which number sentence shows how many days it would take Deepak to walk 27.2 miles?
   Ⓐ $27.2 \times \underline{\hspace{0.7cm}} = 1.6$
   Ⓑ $1.6 \div \underline{\hspace{0.7cm}} = 27.2$
   Ⓒ $27.2 \times 1.6 = \underline{\hspace{0.7cm}}$
   Ⓓ $27.2 \div 1.6 = \underline{\hspace{0.7cm}}$

Word Problems with Functional Relationships

Use the function table to answer the questions below.

1	2	3	4	5
5	10	15	20	25

1. Julie's class made a function table to show how many books they read each month of the year. If the function table starts with September as the first month, how many books did the class read in November?
Ⓐ 5
Ⓑ 10
Ⓒ 15
Ⓓ 20

2. Each student in the class has to tell what the rule of the function table is. Which student response is correct?
Ⓐ add 5
Ⓑ add 10
Ⓒ multiply by 5
Ⓓ multiply by 5 and add 1

3. How many books do you think Julie's class will read in February? Which number sentence shows the answer?
Ⓐ 6 + 30 = 36
Ⓑ 6 × 30 = 180
Ⓒ 6 + 5 = 11
Ⓓ 6 × 5 = 30

4. During which month did Julie's class read 5 more books than the month before?
Ⓐ September
Ⓑ October
Ⓒ December
Ⓓ all of the months

5. How many books will Julie's class read in April?
Ⓐ 35
Ⓑ 45
Ⓒ 40
Ⓓ 50

6. During which two months did Julie's class read 15 books in total?
Ⓐ September and October
Ⓑ October and December
Ⓒ November and January
Ⓓ September and January

Section 6: Measurement and Geometry
Choosing a Measurement Tool or Unit

Answer the questions below.

1. Which tool **best** measures the length of a feather?
   - Ⓐ ruler
   - Ⓑ scale
   - Ⓒ balance
   - Ⓓ hand lens

2. Which unit **best** measures how much milk is in a container?
   - Ⓐ yard
   - Ⓑ inch
   - Ⓒ gallon
   - Ⓓ mile

3. Which unit **best** measures the weight of a child?
   - Ⓐ pound
   - Ⓑ ounce
   - Ⓒ ton
   - Ⓓ none of the above

4. Which unit **best** measures the length of a caterpillar?
   - Ⓐ meter
   - Ⓑ decimeter
   - Ⓒ centimeter
   - Ⓓ millimeter

5. Which tool **best** measures the weight of a piece of fruit?
   - Ⓐ ruler
   - Ⓑ beaker
   - Ⓒ spring scale
   - Ⓓ thermometer

6. Which unit would you use to measure the volume of a pitcher of water?
   - Ⓐ liter
   - Ⓑ milliliter
   - Ⓒ gram
   - Ⓓ milligram

7. Which object would you measure in pounds?
   - Ⓐ a flower
   - Ⓑ a pumpkin
   - Ⓒ a feather
   - Ⓓ a truck

8. Which distance is **best** measured in miles?
   - Ⓐ the distance from one town to another
   - Ⓑ the distance from one desk to another
   - Ⓒ the length of your arm
   - Ⓓ the length of a house

Converting Measurements

Answer the questions below.

1. There are 12 inches in 1 foot. How many inches are in 2 feet?
- Ⓐ 1
- Ⓑ 2
- Ⓒ 12
- Ⓓ 24

2. There are 60 seconds in one minute. How many seconds are in 2 minutes?
- Ⓐ 12
- Ⓑ 30
- Ⓒ 60
- Ⓓ 120

3. There are 60 minutes in one hour. How many minutes are in a half hour?
- Ⓐ 120
- Ⓑ 60
- Ⓒ 30
- Ⓓ 15

4. There are 100 centimeters in one meter. How many centimeters are in 8 meters?
- Ⓐ 8
- Ⓑ 80
- Ⓒ 100
- Ⓓ 800

5. There are 1,000 millimeters in one meter. How many millimeters are in a half a meter?
- Ⓐ 500
- Ⓑ 1,000
- Ⓒ 5,000
- Ⓓ 10,000

6. There are 1,000 milliliters in one liter. How many milliliters are in 4 liters?
- Ⓐ 4
- Ⓑ 40
- Ⓒ 400
- Ⓓ 4,000

7. There are 24 hours in one day. How many hours are in 3 days?
- Ⓐ 8
- Ⓑ 48
- Ⓒ 72
- Ⓓ 96

8. There are 7 days in one week. How many days are there in 2 weeks?
- Ⓐ 14 days
- Ⓑ 14 weeks
- Ⓒ 1 month
- Ⓓ 1 year

9. There are 16 ounces in one pound. How many ounces are in 2 pounds?
- Ⓐ 8
- Ⓑ 16
- Ⓒ 32
- Ⓓ 38

10. There are 2,000 pounds in one ton. How many pounds are in a half ton?
- Ⓐ 4,000
- Ⓑ 2,000
- Ⓒ 1,000
- Ⓓ 5000

Perimeter of Polygons

Answer the questions below.

1. What is the perimeter of the rectangle?

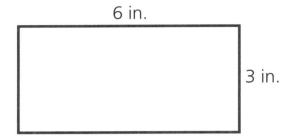

Ⓐ 24 inches
Ⓑ 18 inches
Ⓒ 12 inches
Ⓓ 9 inches

2. What is the perimeter of the triangle?

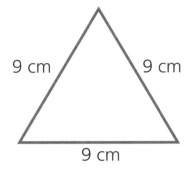

Ⓐ 9 cm
Ⓑ 18 cm
Ⓒ 27 cm
Ⓓ 30 cm

3. What is the perimeter of the square?

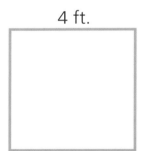

Ⓐ 4 feet
Ⓑ 8 feet
Ⓒ 12 feet
Ⓓ 16 feet

4. What is the perimeter of the figure?

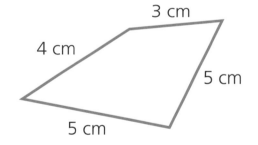

Ⓐ 18 cm
Ⓑ 17 cm
Ⓒ 12 cm
Ⓓ 9 cm

Identifying Polygons

Answer the questions below.

1. Which figure is an octagon?

Ⓐ 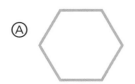   Ⓑ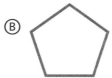

Ⓒ 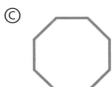   Ⓓ

2. Which figure is shown?

Ⓐ triangle
Ⓑ rhombus
Ⓒ pentagon
Ⓓ trapezoid

3. How many sides does a hexagon have?
Ⓐ 5
Ⓑ 6
Ⓒ 7
Ⓓ 8

4. Which figure is a parallelogram?

Ⓐ    Ⓑ

Ⓒ    Ⓓ

5. How many corners does an oval have?
Ⓐ 0
Ⓑ 2
Ⓒ 3
Ⓓ 4

6. Which figure is shown?

Ⓐ pentagon
Ⓑ octagon
Ⓒ rhombus
Ⓓ circle

Identifying Solid Figures

Answer the questions below.

1. Which figure shows a cylinder?

Ⓐ    Ⓑ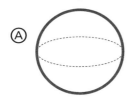

Ⓒ    Ⓓ

2. Which figure has no edges and no faces?

Ⓐ cylinder
Ⓑ sphere
Ⓒ triangular prism
Ⓓ cube

3. Which figure is shown?

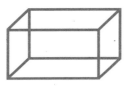

Ⓐ cube
Ⓑ triangular prism
Ⓒ rectangular prism
Ⓓ cone

4. Which figure shows a cone?

Ⓐ 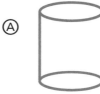   Ⓑ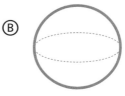

Ⓒ   Ⓓ

5. How many faces does a cube have?

Ⓐ 4
Ⓑ 5
Ⓒ 6
Ⓓ 8

6. Which figure is shown?

Ⓐ rectangular prism
Ⓑ triangular prism
Ⓒ cone
Ⓓ cylinder

Identifying Angles

Answer the questions below.

1. Which angle is a right angle?

2. What kind of angle is shown?

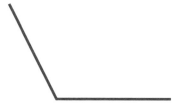

Ⓐ right angle
Ⓑ acute angle
Ⓒ obtuse angle
Ⓓ none of the above

3. What kind of angles make up a square?
Ⓐ right angles
Ⓑ acute angles
Ⓒ obtuse angles
Ⓓ none of the above

4. What kind of angles make up this triangle?
Ⓐ right angles
Ⓑ acute angles
Ⓒ obtuse angles
Ⓓ none of the above

5. Which angle is an acute angle?

6. How many degrees is a right angle?
Ⓐ 45
Ⓑ 90
Ⓒ 180
Ⓓ 360

Classifying Triangles

Answer the questions below.

1. Which is an equilateral triangle?

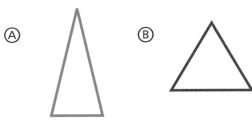

Ⓐ Ⓑ Ⓒ Ⓓ

2. What kind of triangle has one angle that is 90 degrees?
Ⓐ isosceles triangle
Ⓑ equilateral triangle
Ⓒ scalene triangle
Ⓓ right triangle

3. What kind of triangle is shown?

Ⓐ scalene triangle
Ⓑ equilateral triangle
Ⓒ isosceles triangle
Ⓓ right triangle

4. Which kind of triangle has two angles that are the same degrees?
Ⓐ scalene triangle
Ⓑ equilateral triangle
Ⓒ isosceles triangle
Ⓓ right triangle

5. What kind of triangle is shown?

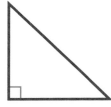

Ⓐ isosceles triangle
Ⓑ right triangle
Ⓒ scalene triangle
Ⓓ equilateral triangle

6. Which shows an isosceles triangle?

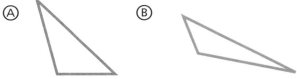

Ⓐ Ⓑ Ⓒ Ⓓ

Section 7: Statistics, Data Analysis, and Probability
Certain, Likely, Improbable, and Impossible

Use the picture to answer questions 1–3.

1. What is the likelihood that a black ball
will be pulled from the bag?
Ⓐ certain
Ⓑ likely
Ⓒ improbable
Ⓓ impossible

2. What is the likelihood that a white ball
will be pulled from the bag?
Ⓐ certain
Ⓑ likely
Ⓒ improbable
Ⓓ impossible

3. What is the likelihood that a green ball
will be pulled from the bag?
Ⓐ certain
Ⓑ likely
Ⓒ improbable
Ⓓ impossible

Use the picture to answer questions 4–6.

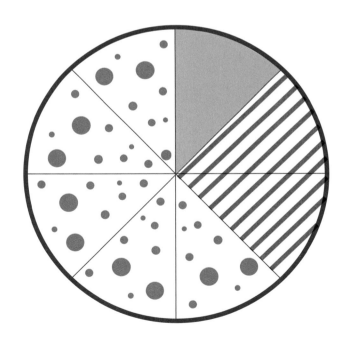

4. What is the likelihood that the spinner
will land on black?
Ⓐ certain
Ⓑ likely
Ⓒ improbable
Ⓓ impossible

5. What is the likelihood that the spinner
will land on gray?
Ⓐ certain
Ⓑ likely
Ⓒ improbable
Ⓓ impossible

6. What is the likelihood that the spinner
will land on polka dots?
Ⓐ certain
Ⓑ likely
Ⓒ improbable
Ⓓ impossible

Likelihood of Everyday Events

Answer the questions below.

1. What is the likelihood of walking across the ocean tomorrow?
- Ⓐ certain
- Ⓑ likely
- Ⓒ improbable
- Ⓓ impossible

2. What is the likelihood that the sun will rise tomorrow?
- Ⓐ certain
- Ⓑ likely
- Ⓒ improbable
- Ⓓ impossible

3. What is the likelihood that you will see a car today?
- Ⓐ certain
- Ⓑ likely
- Ⓒ improbable
- Ⓓ impossible

4. What is the likelihood that you will burn your hand if you touch a cup of hot chocolate?
- Ⓐ certain
- Ⓑ likely
- Ⓒ improbable
- Ⓓ impossible

Use the table to answer questions 5–8.

1	3	5
7	9	7
5	3	1

5. You drop a pebble on the chart. What is the likelihood that the pebble will land on an odd number?
- Ⓐ certain
- Ⓑ likely
- Ⓒ improbable
- Ⓓ impossible

6. What is the likelihood that the pebble will land on a number higher than 10?
- Ⓐ certain
- Ⓑ likely
- Ⓒ improbable
- Ⓓ impossible

7. What is the likelihood that the pebble will land on one of the first two rows of the chart?
- Ⓐ certain
- Ⓑ likely
- Ⓒ improbable
- Ⓓ impossible

8. What is the likelihood that the pebble will land on the number 5?
- Ⓐ certain
- Ⓑ likely
- Ⓒ improbable
- Ⓓ impossible

More Likely, Less Likely, Equally Likely

Use the picture to answer the questions below.

1. You close your eyes and pick one crayon from the box. Which color crayon is **most likely** to be chosen?
   Ⓐ brown
   Ⓑ orange
   Ⓒ red
   Ⓓ yellow

2. Which two crayon colors are **equally likely** to be chosen?
   Ⓐ yellow and red
   Ⓑ red and orange
   Ⓒ orange and brown
   Ⓓ brown and red

3. You choose two yellow crayons. What are the chances that you will choose a yellow, red, or orange crayon the next time you choose?
   Ⓐ not likely
   Ⓑ less likely
   Ⓒ more likely
   Ⓓ equally likely

4. Which crayon color are you **least likely** to choose from the box?
   Ⓐ brown
   Ⓑ orange
   Ⓒ red
   Ⓓ yellow

5. Which crayon color is **less likely** than red to be chosen?
   Ⓐ yellow
   Ⓑ orange
   Ⓒ brown
   Ⓓ none of the crayons

6. Which crayon color is **equally likely** as yellow to be chosen?
   Ⓐ red
   Ⓑ orange
   Ⓒ brown
   Ⓓ none of the crayons

Tally Charts

Use the tally chart below to answer questions 1–4.

Favorite Colors

blue	⊮⊮ ll
green	⊮⊮
red	llll

1. Inez's class took a vote of their favorite colors. How many students are in Inez's class?
   Ⓐ 4
   Ⓑ 5
   Ⓒ 7
   Ⓓ 16

2. Which color is the least favorite of the students in the class?
   Ⓐ red
   Ⓑ blue
   Ⓒ green
   Ⓓ cannot tell

3. Which color got 5 votes from the students in the class?
   Ⓐ red
   Ⓑ blue
   Ⓒ green
   Ⓓ cannot tell

4. Which color did Inez vote for?
   Ⓐ red
   Ⓑ blue
   Ⓒ green
   Ⓓ cannot tell

Use the tally chart below to answer questions 5–6.

Favorite Snacks

popcorn	⊮⊮ lll
pretzels	⊮⊮ l
nuts	⊮⊮
crackers	⊮⊮

5. Sun's class voted for their favorite snacks. Which two snacks had the same number of votes?
   Ⓐ popcorn and pretzels
   Ⓑ nuts and crackers
   Ⓒ popcorn and crackers
   Ⓓ pretzels and nuts

6. Which snack had the most votes?
   Ⓐ popcorn
   Ⓑ pretzels
   Ⓒ nuts
   Ⓓ crackers

Bar Graphs

The bar graph shows the number of all third grade students who own pets.
Use the bar graph to answer the questions below.

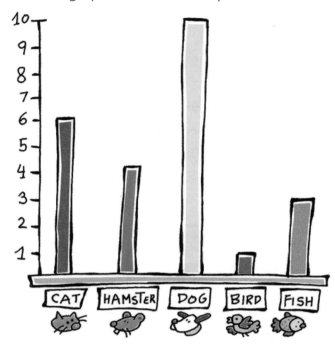

1. How many pet owners took the survey?
   Ⓐ 18
   Ⓑ 22
   Ⓒ 24
   Ⓓ 30

2. Which pet was owned by 3 students?
   Ⓐ cat
   Ⓑ hamster
   Ⓒ bird
   Ⓓ fish

3. Which pet was owned by the most number of students?
   Ⓐ cat
   Ⓑ dog
   Ⓒ hamster
   Ⓓ fish

4. How many students own cats?
   Ⓐ 3
   Ⓑ 4
   Ⓒ 6
   Ⓓ 10

5. How many students own hamsters?
   Ⓐ 3
   Ⓑ 4
   Ⓒ 6
   Ⓓ 10

6. How many more students own hamsters than birds?
   Ⓐ 1
   Ⓑ 2
   Ⓒ 3
   Ⓓ 4

Line Plots

The line plot shows the ages of students on the soccer team.
Use the line plot to answer the questions below.

AGES OF STUDENTS ON SOCCER TEAM

1. What is the age range of students on the soccer team?
   Ⓐ 8–12
   Ⓑ 8–11
   Ⓒ 9–10
   Ⓓ 9–12

2. How many students on the soccer team are 11 years old?
   Ⓐ 0
   Ⓑ 2
   Ⓒ 4
   Ⓓ 7

3. What age is the greatest number of students on the team?
   Ⓐ 12
   Ⓑ 11
   Ⓒ 10
   Ⓓ 9

4. How many 10 and 11 year olds are on the team?
   Ⓐ 9
   Ⓑ 7
   Ⓒ 6
   Ⓓ 4

5. How many 8 and 9 year olds are on the team?
   Ⓐ 4
   Ⓑ 6
   Ⓒ 7
   Ⓓ 9

6. How many students are on the team in all?
   Ⓐ 7
   Ⓑ 12
   Ⓒ 14
   Ⓓ 15

Recording Data

Answer the questions below.

1. You toss a coin 5 times. Which tally chart shows the possible outcomes of the coin toss?

Ⓐ
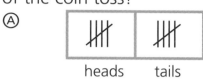
heads   tails

Ⓑ
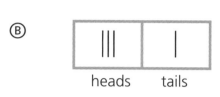
heads   tails

Ⓒ
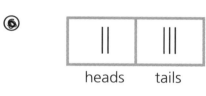
heads   tails

Ⓓ
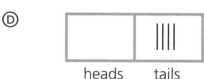
heads   tails

2. What would be a good title for this bar graph?

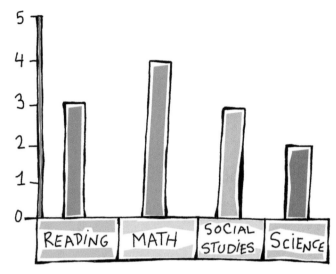

Ⓐ People Who Like Reading
Ⓑ People in My Class
Ⓒ Favorite School Subjects
Ⓓ Favorite Social Studies Topics

3. Which kind of chart would be **best** for recording the number of students in your classroom?
Ⓐ tally chart
Ⓑ bar graph
Ⓒ line plot
Ⓓ pie chart

4. Which kind of chart would be **best** for displaying the ages of the people in your class?
Ⓐ tally chart
Ⓑ bar graph
Ⓒ line plot
Ⓓ pie chart

Section 8: Mathematical Reasoning

Rounding

Answer the questions below.

1. Which number shows 5,466 rounded to the nearest hundred?
   Ⓐ 5,000
   Ⓑ 5,400
   Ⓒ 5,500
   Ⓓ 5,600

2. Which number shows 799 rounded to the nearest hundred?
   Ⓐ 900
   Ⓑ 800
   Ⓒ 780
   Ⓓ 700

3. Which number shows 18 rounded to the nearest ten?
   Ⓐ 10
   Ⓑ 15
   Ⓒ 18
   Ⓓ 20

4. Which number shows 74,500 rounded to the nearest ten thousand?
   Ⓐ 80,000
   Ⓑ 75,000
   Ⓒ 74,000
   Ⓓ 70,000

5. Which number shows 8,435,977 rounded to the nearest million?
   Ⓐ 8,000,000
   Ⓑ 8,500,000
   Ⓒ 8,400,000
   Ⓓ 9,000,000

6. Which number shows 75,999 rounded to the nearest thousand?
   Ⓐ 75,000
   Ⓑ 76,000
   Ⓒ 78,000
   Ⓓ 80,000

7. Which number shows 73 rounded to the nearest ten?
   Ⓐ 100
   Ⓑ 80
   Ⓒ 75
   Ⓓ 70

8. Which number shows 324 rounded to the nearest hundred?
   Ⓐ 200
   Ⓑ 300
   Ⓒ 400
   Ⓓ 500

9. Which number shows 8,334 rounded to the nearest hundred?
Ⓐ 8,000
Ⓑ 8,330
Ⓒ 8,300
Ⓓ 8,400

10. Which number shows 27,675 rounded to the nearest thousand?
Ⓐ 27,000
Ⓑ 27,500
Ⓒ 27,600
Ⓓ 28,000

11. Which number shows 4,367,998 rounded to the nearest million?
Ⓐ 4,300,000
Ⓑ 4,000,000
Ⓒ 4,367,000
Ⓓ 5,000,000

12. Which number shows 3,675 rounded to the nearest ten?
Ⓐ 3,680
Ⓑ 3,600
Ⓒ 3,670
Ⓓ 4,000

13. Which number shows 89,250 rounded to the nearest hundred?
Ⓐ 89,000
Ⓑ 90,000
Ⓒ 89,200
Ⓓ 89,300

14. Which number shows 2,348,226 rounded to the nearest thousand?
Ⓐ 2,348,000
Ⓑ 2,348,200
Ⓒ 2,300,000
Ⓓ 2,400,000

15. Which number shows 556,368 rounded to the nearest ten thousand?
Ⓐ 556,000
Ⓑ 560,000
Ⓒ 550,000
Ⓓ 556,300

16. Which number shows 9,332 rounded to the nearest ten?
Ⓐ 9,340
Ⓑ 9,000
Ⓒ 9,340
Ⓓ 9,330

Estimating

Answer the questions below.

1. Estimate to the nearest ten.

$$56 + 30 =$$

Ⓐ 70
Ⓑ 80
Ⓒ 90
Ⓓ 100

2. Estimate to the nearest hundred.

$$803 \times 2 =$$

Ⓐ 2,000
Ⓑ 1,600
Ⓒ 1,500
Ⓓ 1,000

3. Estimate to the nearest ten.

$$63 \div 6 =$$

Ⓐ 9
Ⓑ 10
Ⓒ 15
Ⓓ 20

4. Estimate to the nearest thousand.

$$7,800 + 4,300 =$$

Ⓐ 14,000
Ⓑ 13,000
Ⓒ 12,000
Ⓓ 11,000

5. Estimate to the nearest ten.

$$80 \times 31 =$$

Ⓐ 3,000
Ⓑ 2,500
Ⓒ 2,400
Ⓓ 2,300

6. Estimate to the nearest ten.

$$100 \div 52 =$$

Ⓐ 52
Ⓑ 20
Ⓒ 50
Ⓓ 2

7. Estimate to the nearest thousand.

$$8,035 - 7,455 =$$

Ⓐ 1,000
Ⓑ 2,000
Ⓒ 3,000
Ⓓ 4,000

8. Estimate to the nearest thousand.

$$3,699 - 2,986 =$$

Ⓐ 4,000
Ⓑ 3,000
Ⓒ 1,000
Ⓓ 500

Estimating Word Problems

Answer the questions below.

1. Seth collected about 1,000 stamps. He gave approximately 350 of them to his sister. Which number shows the closest estimate of the number of stamps Seth has left in his collection?
Ⓐ 300
Ⓑ 400
Ⓒ 500
Ⓓ 600

2. Mr. Shoki planted 88 tulips and 72 marigolds in his garden. Which number shows an estimate of the number of total plants Mr. Shoki put in the garden?
Ⓐ 180
Ⓑ 160
Ⓒ 150
Ⓓ 100

3. Sol walked 19 miles last week. Which number shows approximately half the number of miles that Sol walked?
Ⓐ 20
Ⓑ 15
Ⓒ 10
Ⓓ 5

4. Each student in Nikki's class answered about 12 questions on the test. There are 8 students in the class. About how many questions were answered in all?
Ⓐ 200
Ⓑ 150
Ⓒ 100
Ⓓ 50

5. Dayna saved 63 pennies and 29 nickels. About how many coins does she have in all?
Ⓐ 70
Ⓑ 80
Ⓒ 90
Ⓓ 100

6. Rashid does 19 jumping jacks per day for 15 days. About how many jumping jacks does he do in total?
Ⓐ 150
Ⓑ 200
Ⓒ 250
Ⓓ 300

Estimating or Finding the Exact Answer

Choose whether an estimate or the exact answer is needed for each of the problems below.

1. Heidi has to hand out drinks to each runner in a race. There are 467 runners. Each runner needs 3 cups of water. Each runner needs enough water. Should Heidi estimate or find the exact number of cups of water needed?
   Ⓐ estimate
   Ⓑ find the exact number
   Ⓒ neither estimate nor find the exact number
   Ⓓ It does not matter.

2. There are 4,682 balloons at the circus. About half the balloons should be on the stage, and half should be in the audience. Should the circus workers estimate or find the exact number of balloons for each location?
   Ⓐ estimate
   Ⓑ find the exact number
   Ⓒ neither estimate nor find the exact number
   Ⓓ It does not matter.

3. Jack sold 57 glasses of lemonade at $1 per glass. He wants to buy a game that costs $50. Does Jack need an estimate or an exact amount to tell whether he has sold enough lemonade to buy the game?
   Ⓐ estimate
   Ⓑ find the exact amount
   Ⓒ neither estimate nor find the exact amount
   Ⓓ It does not matter.

4. Samuel picked about 30 apples from his apple tree. He is bringing an apple for each of his classmates. In order for Samuel to bring enough apples to school, does he need an estimate or an exact count of the number of apples he has?
   Ⓐ estimate
   Ⓑ find the exact count
   Ⓒ neither estimate nor find the exact count
   Ⓓ It does not matter.

Checking for Reasonableness

Answer the questions below.

1. Sara, Kari, and Shawna are going to the movies. It costs about $7.50 per person to see the movie. The girls decide that they need to bring $18 for their tickets. Is their estimate reasonable?

Ⓐ no
Ⓑ Yes, they have just the right amount.
Ⓒ Yes, but they will have very little left over for snacks.
Ⓓ Yes, and they will have a lot of money left over for snacks.

2. Lee's class earned about $500 at the school bake sale. They want to buy 20 books that cost about $10 each. They think they have enough to buy the books. Is their estimate reasonable?

Ⓐ no
Ⓑ Yes, they have just the right amount.
Ⓒ Yes, but they will have very little left over.
Ⓓ Yes, and they will have a lot of money left over.

3. The Rodriquez family wants to make a goodie bag for each student in the school. They estimated that they will have to make 200 goodie bags. There are about 20 students in each of the 12 classes at the school. Was their estimate reasonable?

Ⓐ no
Ⓑ Yes, they estimated just the right amount.
Ⓒ Yes, but they will have very few bags left over.
Ⓓ Yes, and they will have a lot of bags left over.

4. Jesse has to read a 300-page book in 15 days. He estimates that he must read about 22 pages a day. Is his estimate reasonable?

Ⓐ no
Ⓑ Yes, he will finish the book right on time.
Ⓒ Yes, but he will finish the book a little bit earlier than planned.
Ⓓ Yes, but he will finish the book a lot earlier than planned.

Too Much, Not Enough Information

Answer the questions below to tell if the word problems give too much information, not enough information, or just the right amount of information to solve the problem.

1. Caleb swam 24 laps on Monday, 30 laps on Tuesday, and 18 laps on Thursday. How many laps did Caleb swim during the whole week?
   Ⓐ too much information
   Ⓑ not enough information
   Ⓒ just the right amount of information
   Ⓓ none of the above

The chart shows how many handmade necklaces Abby sold. Use the chart to answer questions 2–5.

Month	Number of Necklaces Sold
January	17
February	20
March	16
April	18
May	22

2. How many necklaces did Abby sell in January and February?
   Ⓐ too much information
   Ⓑ not enough information
   Ⓒ just the right amount of information
   Ⓓ none of the above

3. How many necklaces did Abby sell in June?
   Ⓐ too much information
   Ⓑ not enough information
   Ⓒ just the right amount of information
   Ⓓ none of the above

4. How many necklaces did Abby sell in January through May?
   Ⓐ too much information
   Ⓑ not enough information
   Ⓒ just the right amount of information
   Ⓓ none of the above

5. How many more necklaces does Abby need to sell to make $100?
   Ⓐ too much information
   Ⓑ not enough information
   Ⓒ just the right amount of information
   Ⓓ none of the above

Choosing the Operation

Choose the operation needed to solve each word problem below.

1. Olivia collected 482 stickers. She gave 50 to her cousin. How many stickers did Olivia have left in her collection?
Ⓐ addition
Ⓑ subtraction
Ⓒ multiplication
Ⓓ division

2. Miguel went to the store counter with items that cost $15, $2.25, $6.20, $21, and $3.75. How much did Miguel spend in all?
Ⓐ addition
Ⓑ subtraction
Ⓒ multiplication
Ⓓ division

3. Anna picked 38 apples. She had exactly enough to give 2 apples to each classmate. How many classmates does Anna have?
Ⓐ addition
Ⓑ subtraction
Ⓒ multiplication
Ⓓ division

4. Gregory has 17 pretzels. Each of his 4 friends has the same amount of pretzels. How many pretzels do all of the children have?
Ⓐ addition
Ⓑ subtraction
Ⓒ multiplication
Ⓓ division

5. Salah walked 15 blocks to the movie theater, then 12 more blocks to the store. How many blocks did he walk in all?
Ⓐ addition
Ⓑ subtraction
Ⓒ multiplication
Ⓓ division

6. Mr. Samuels has 144 stickers. He wants to give an equal number to 12 students. How many will he give to each student?
Ⓐ addition
Ⓑ subtraction
Ⓒ multiplication
Ⓓ division

Elapsed Time

Answer the questions below.

1. Lunch starts at 1:00. It ends at 1:20. How long is lunch?
Ⓐ 1 hour
Ⓑ 20 minutes
Ⓒ 15 minutes
Ⓓ 10 minutes

2. The movie is 2 hours long. It starts at 4:40. When does it end?
Ⓐ 2:40
Ⓑ 4:40
Ⓒ 6:40
Ⓓ 7:00

3. Each reading class is 15 minutes long. How long do 4 reading classes take?
Ⓐ 15 minutes
Ⓑ 30 minutes
Ⓒ 45 minutes
Ⓓ 1 hour

4. The cake must bake for 50 minutes. It went in the oven at 2:30. When should it come out?
Ⓐ 2:40
Ⓑ 2:50
Ⓒ 3:20
Ⓓ 3:25

5. The party starts at 3:00. It lasts 2 and a half hours. When will the party end?
Ⓐ 4:30
Ⓑ 5:00
Ⓒ 5:30
Ⓓ 6:00

6. Jackie went into the store at 5:40. She came out at 6:15. How long was she in the store?
Ⓐ 25 minutes
Ⓑ 35 minutes
Ⓒ 45 minutes
Ⓓ 55 minutes

7. School starts at 8:30. Lunch is at 11:30. How many hours of school are there before lunch?
Ⓐ 2 hours
Ⓑ 2 hours and 20 minutes
Ⓒ 3 hours
Ⓓ 3 hours and 20 minutes

8. It took Dominick 45 minutes to do his homework. He started at 4:00. When did he finish?
Ⓐ 4:00
Ⓑ 4:15
Ⓒ 4:45
Ⓓ 5:45

9. Yamil rode her bike for 30 minutes. She finished at 4:25. When did she start?
Ⓐ 3:00
Ⓑ 3:55
Ⓒ 4:00
Ⓓ 4:30

10. It takes 75 minutes to get to Cousin Brooke's house. If we leave at noon, what time will we arrive?
Ⓐ 1:15
Ⓑ 1:00
Ⓒ 12:45
Ⓓ 12:30

11. Mom started to cook dinner at 5:10. It took her an hour and twenty minutes to finish dinner. What time was she done?
Ⓐ 5:45
Ⓑ 5:30
Ⓒ 6:00
Ⓓ 6:30

12. Roberto played basketball from 5:00 to 6:55. For how long did he play?
Ⓐ 2 hours
Ⓑ 1 hour and a half
Ⓒ 55 minutes
Ⓓ 1 hour and 55 minutes

13. It took Beverly two hours and five minutes to finish her homework assignment. She began working at 3:30. What time did she finish?
Ⓐ 5:00
Ⓑ 6:05
Ⓒ 5:35
Ⓓ 5:30

14. Max and Milo's chess game began at 10:35 and ended at 12:00. How long was the chess game?
Ⓐ 1 hour and 25 minutes
Ⓑ 1 hour and 45 minutes
Ⓒ 2 hours
Ⓓ 1 hour and 30 minutes

15. The TV show starts at 7:30. It is 2 hours long. What time does it end?
Ⓐ 8:45
Ⓑ 8:30
Ⓒ 9:00
Ⓓ 9:30

16. We arrived at the zoo at 10:15 and stayed until 5:00. How much time did we spend at the zoo?
Ⓐ 7 hours
Ⓑ 6 hours and 45 minutes
Ⓒ 6 hours and 30 minutes
Ⓓ 7 hours and 45 minutes

Section 9: Test

Answer the questions below.

1. 73 + 81 =
Ⓐ 154
Ⓑ 157
Ⓒ 164
Ⓓ 167

2. 349 − 39 =
Ⓐ 320
Ⓑ 310
Ⓒ 308
Ⓓ 301

3. 72 × 8 =
Ⓐ 446
Ⓑ 552
Ⓒ 567
Ⓓ 576

4. 92 ÷ 3 =
Ⓐ 30
Ⓑ 30R1
Ⓒ 30R2
Ⓓ 31

5. 36.92 + 27.44 =
Ⓐ 63.73
Ⓑ 64.36
Ⓒ 64.66
Ⓓ 64.79

6. $\frac{1}{4}$ + $\frac{2}{4}$ =
Ⓐ $\frac{3}{4}$
Ⓑ $\frac{4}{4}$
Ⓒ $\frac{2}{3}$
Ⓓ $\frac{1}{3}$

7. Which number sentence is correct?
Ⓐ 54.3 < 56.7
Ⓑ 82.11 < 11.82
Ⓒ 90.01 > 90.10
Ⓓ 37.24 > 74.22

8. Which numbers are listed from least to greatest?
Ⓐ 1,300, 1,400, 1,500, 600
Ⓑ 734, 756, 822, 811
Ⓒ 8,322, 8,466, 8,233, 8,644
Ⓓ 8,233, 8,322, 8,466, 8,644

9. Which operation completes the number sentence?

$$834 \_\_\_\_ 234 = 600$$

Ⓐ +

Ⓑ −

Ⓒ ×

Ⓓ ÷

10. Which property does the number sentence show?

$$5 \times (9 \times 2) = (5 \times 9) \times 2$$

Ⓐ Distributive

Ⓑ Commutative

Ⓒ Associative

Ⓓ Identity

11. Which unit would **best** measure the weight of a sandwich?

Ⓐ pound

Ⓑ ounce

Ⓒ ton

Ⓓ mile

12. Which tool would **best** measure the temperature of an oven?

Ⓐ ruler

Ⓑ measuring cup

Ⓒ balance

Ⓓ thermometer

13. There are 12 inches in one foot. How many inches are in 4 feet?

Ⓐ 32 inches

Ⓑ 38 inches

Ⓒ 48 inches

Ⓓ 52 inches

14. Which figure has 5 sides?

Ⓐ octagon

Ⓑ pentagon

Ⓒ hexagon

Ⓓ rhombus

15. Which figure is shown?

Ⓐ cylinder

Ⓑ sphere

Ⓒ cone

Ⓓ triangular prism

16. Which angle has more than 90 degrees but less than 180 degrees?

Ⓐ triangle

Ⓑ obtuse

Ⓒ acute

Ⓓ right

17. What is the perimeter of the figure?

Ⓐ 7 cm
Ⓑ 8 cm
Ⓒ 9 cm
Ⓓ 12 cm

2 cm
4 cm
3 cm
3 cm

18. Which figure shows an obtuse angle?

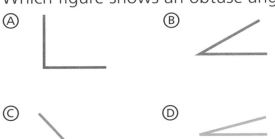

Ⓐ　　Ⓑ

Ⓒ　　Ⓓ

19. What kind of triangle is shown?

Ⓐ right triangle
Ⓑ equilateral triangle
Ⓒ scalene triangle
Ⓓ isosceles triangle

20. What are the chances that Tara will pick a goldfish from the bag?

Ⓐ certain
Ⓑ likely
Ⓒ improbable
Ⓓ impossible

21. Which color marker would it be impossible for Andre to choose?

Ⓐ blue
Ⓑ red
Ⓒ black
Ⓓ green

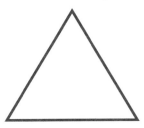

22. The tally chart shows the number of students who bought lunch today. How many students bought lunch?

Ⓐ 3
Ⓑ 5
Ⓒ 6
Ⓓ 11

23. The line plot shows the test scores of students in the class. How many students scored an 89 on their test?

Ⓐ 2
Ⓑ 3
Ⓒ 7
Ⓓ 8

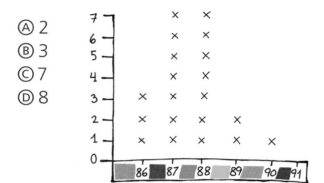

24. Which number shows 4,629 rounded to the nearest thousand?

Ⓐ 4,600
Ⓑ 4,630
Ⓒ 4,700
Ⓓ 5,000

25. Estimate to the nearest hundred.

$$833 + 422 =$$

Ⓐ 1,100
Ⓑ 1,200
Ⓒ 1,300
Ⓓ 1,400

26. Estimate to the nearest ten.

$$249 \times 3 =$$

Ⓐ 740
Ⓑ 745
Ⓒ 750
Ⓓ 755

27. Julia buys a cup of juice every day, Monday through Friday. How much does Julia spend on juice each week?

Ⓐ $5.00
Ⓑ $4.00
Ⓒ There is too much information.
Ⓓ There is not enough information to solve the problem.

28. Max walks about 7 miles each week. About how many weeks will it take him to walk 70 miles?

Ⓐ 1 week
Ⓑ 10 weeks
Ⓒ 100 days
Ⓓ 100 weeks

Answer Key

Page 8
1. C
2. B
3. D
4. B

Page 9
1. D
2. D
3. B
4. C

Page 10
1. A
2. B
3. C
4. B

Page 11
1. C
2. D
3. B
4. C

Page 12
1. B
2. B
3. C
4. A

Page 13
1. B
2. B
3. A
4. D

Page 14
1. C
2. B
3. D
4. B

Page 15
1. A
2. D
3. B
4. B

Page 16
1. C
2. D
3. A
4. C

Page 17
1. D
2. B
3. B
4. C

Page 18
1. C
2. C
3. C
4. D

Page 19
1. C
2. B
3. D
4. B

Page 20
1. D
2. B
3. C
4. B

Page 21
1. A
2. B
3. D
4. B

Page 22
1. C
2. D
3. A
4. A

Page 23
1. B
2. A
3. C
4. C

Page 24
1. B
2. A
3. D
4. C

Page 25
1. D
2. D
3. B
4. A

Page 26
1. D
2. C
3. C
4. A

Page 27
1. C
2. B
3. B
4. B
5. A
6. C
7. A
8. A
9. B
10. C

Page 28
1. A
2. C
3. C
4. A
5. B
6. B
7. C
8. D
9. B
10. C

Page 29
1. C
2. B
3. D
4. A
5. D
6. A
7. C
8. C
9. D
10. A

Page 30
1. A
2. C
3. D
4. D
5. D
6. C
7. C
8. C
9. D
10. C

Page 31
1. C
2. A
3. D
4. D
5. B
6. B
7. B
8. C
9. B
10. C

Page 32
1. C
2. D
3. A
4. C
5. D
6. B
7. A
8. C

Page 33
1. C
2. D
3. C
4. C
5. D
6. C
7. A
8. B

Page 34
1. C
2. C
3. C
4. D
5. D
6. A
7. D
8. B
9. A
10. C

Page 35
1. B
2. A
3. C
4. D
5. B
6. C
7. A
8. C
9. C
10. A

Page 36
1. B
2. A
3. C
4. C
5. B
6. C
7. C
8. C
9. B
10. C

Page 37
1. D
2. B
3. C
4. B
5. A
6. D
7. B
8. C
9. D
10. A

Page 38
1. A
2. C
3. D
4. A
5. C
6. A
7. D
8. B
9. D
10. C

Page 39
1. B
2. C
3. D
4. B
5. D
6. A
7. B
8. D
9. B
10. A

Page 40
1. B
2. C
3. C
4. C
5. A
6. B
7. D
8. C
9. C
10. B

Page 41
1. A
2. B
3. D
4. C
5. C
6. D
7. B
8. B
9. A
10. A

Page 42
1. C
2. D
3. B
4. D
5. A
6. B
7. C
8. C
9. A
10. D

Page 43
1. B
2. D
3. C
4. A
5. C
6. A
7. A
8. B
9. D
10. C

Page 44
1. B
2. A
3. D
4. C
5. A
6. D
7. D
8. B
9. A
10. C

Page 45
1. C
2. C
3. A
4. A
5. D
6. B

Pages 46–49
1. C
2. B
3. C
4. A
5. A
6. D
7. D
8. A
9. A
10. B
11. B
12. B
13. D
14. C
15. C
16. D
17. B
18. C
19. C
20. D
21. B
22. A
23. A
24. C
25. C
26. D
27. B
28. C
29. B
30. D
31. D
32. C

Page 50
1. D
2. B
3. A
4. D
5. A
6. C
7. B
8. C
9. C
10. D

Page 51
1. D
2. D
3. B
4. A
5. D
6. B
7. B
8. A
9. A
10. B

Page 52
1. B
2. C
3. A
4. C
5. B

6. A
7. C
8. B
9. A
10. D
11. C
12. A

Page 53
1. B
2. A
3. C
4. A
5. B
6. C
7. D
8. B
9. C
10. A
11. C
12. B

Page 54
1. C
2. A
3. B
4. B
5. D
6. D
7. B
8. A
9. B
10. D
11. C
12. A

Page 55
1. B
2. A
3. D
4. B
5. D
6. C

Page 56
1. B
2. A
3. D
4. C
5. D
6. C

Page 57
1. A
2. D
3. C
4. A
5. B
6. C
7. D
8. C
9. D
10. A

Page 58
1. B
2. C
3. C
4. B
5. B
6. D
7. D
8. C

Page 59
1. C
2. A
3. B
4. D
5. C
6. A
7. B
8. D
9. C
10. B

Page 60
1. D
2. B
3. A
4. C
5. D
6. C
7. A
8. C
9. D
10. B

Page 61
1. B
2. A
3. A
4. C
5. A
6. B
7. C
8. A
9. D
10. B

Page 62
1. B
2. B
3. C
4. D
5. C
6. B
7. C
8. D

Page 63
1. A
2. D
3. B
4. A
5. C
6. B
7. C
8. A
9. B
10. D

Page 64
1. C
2. C
3. D
4. C
5. B
6. D

Page 65
1. C
2. C
3. D
4. D
5. C
6. A

Page 66
1. A
2. C
3. A
4. C
5. C
6. A
7. B
8. A

Page 67
1. D
2. D
3. C
4. D
5. A
6. D
7. C
8. A
9. C
10. C

Page 68
1. B
2. C
3. D
4. B

Page 69
1. C
2. D
3. B
4. D
5. A
6. A

Page 70
1. C
2. C
3. C
4. D
5. C
6. B

Page 71
1. B
2. C
3. A
4. B
5. C
6. B

Page 72
1. B
2. D
3. A
4. C
5. B
6. C

Page 73
1. B
2. C
3. D
4. D
5. C
6. B

Page 74
1. D
2. A
3. B
4. C
5. A
6. D
7. B
8. C

Page 75
1. D
2. B
3. D
4. A
5. C
6. D

Page 76
1. D
2. A
3. C
4. D
5. B
6. A

Page 77
1. C
2. D
3. B
4. C
5. B
6. C

Page 78
1. B
2. B
3. C
4. A
5. B
6. D

Page 79
1. C
2. C
3. A
4. C

Pages 80–81
1. C
2. B
3. D
4. D
5. A
6. B
7. D
8. B
9. C
10. D
11. B
12. A
13. D

14. A
15. B
16. D

Page 82
1. C
2. B
3. B
4. C
5. C
6. D
7. A
8. C

Page 83
1. D
2. B
3. C
4. C
5. C
6. D

Page 84
1. B
2. A
3. B
4. B

Page 85
1. A
2. D
3. A
4. C

Page 86
1. B
2. A
3. B
4. C
5. B

Page 87
1. B
2. A
3. D
4. C
5. A
6. D

Pages 88–89
1. B
2. C
3. D
4. C
5. C
6. B
7. C
8. C
9. B
10. A
11. D
12. D
13. C
14. A
15. D
16. B

Pages 90–93
1. A
2. B
3. D
4. C
5. B
6. A
7. A
8. D
9. B
10. C
11. B
12. D
13. C
14. B
15. C
16. B
17. D
18. C
19. B
20. B
21. D
22. D
23. A
24. D
25. B
26. C
27. D
28. B